BRIAN MAY'S
RED SPECIAL

THIS IS A CARLTON BOOK

This edition published by Carlton Books Limited
20 Mortimer Street
London W1T 3JW

A CIP Catalogue record for this book is available from the British Library

ISBN 978 1 78097 276 3

Printed and bound in Dubai

10 9 8 7 6 5 4 3 2

Overleaf: Brian on stage with Roger Taylor during the Queen+Adam Lambert US tour, June 16, 2014, Burbank California.

BRIAN MAY'S RED SPECIAL

THE STORY OF THE HOME-MADE GUITAR THAT ROCKED QUEEN AND THE WORLD

BRIAN MAY
WITH SIMON BRADLEY

CARLTON
BOOKS

CONTENTS

FOREWORD

This book about my home-made guitar has been waiting in the wings for a very long time. As far back as 1990, I assembled some material for such a tome, having been approached by a publisher to create a book on the design and construction of the 'Red Special'. But the project didn't get very far – we were all too busy just making music.

Much more recently the discussion was renewed, and my venerable old friend Simon Bradley, an experienced writer on rock music and its associated hardware, volunteered to take up the challenge of making the book happen. In a different world, I would have sat down for a year or so and done the job myself, with just a little help from my friends, in the way that I usually write books – 100 per cent hands-on. But the world I now inhabit is now more frenetic than ever, and it had become clearer and clearer that, left in my hands, the book would never materialise. So I'm very grateful to Simon for diving in, doing his homework, including interviewing me at length to get my input, and driving this thing all the way to the chequered flag. The book has undoubtedly grown a new dimension because of Simon's informed overview and the energy he has put in. It has also been good for me to learn to let go a little.

It was Simon's decision to present the major part of the book in interview format, to maintain its informal feel. I've just revisited the text and done some polishing and clarification, and filling in some of some of the gaps I left in the interviews, but on the whole, in flicking through these pages, you are essentially reading a spontaneous conversation between Simon and myself. So we make no claims that the book is rigorous in its order of presentation, or complete as regards to answering all the questions that can be asked about the guitar. But I do feel that Simon has built something that is entertaining to anyone interested in this story, and informative in a light and accessible way. The team has also done a great job in assembling the pictures to bring the story to life, many of which were long forgotten by us all, especially me!

Over the years I've answered a multitude of technical and other questions on my website platform – 'Brian's Soapbox' at www.brianmay.com. If, after reading this book, you have a question or comment, please feel free to email me there, and I'll do my best to answer. In fact, when this book is published we might just make a special place on site to collect all this dialogue. But you can always find me at www.brianmay.com. If you want more information about the guitars we make and supply, as Brian May Guitars (BMG), there is a website for this also, at www.brianmayguitars.co.uk.

As I write this foreword, I'm on a major tour of the USA as Queen + Adam Lambert. We just played the Los Angeles Forum, packed out and rockin' again after a gap of over 30 years. The excitement and the roar of approval have been just as stimulating as in the Old Days, and my old companion the Red Special has been in particularly good voice and as much a part of me as ever. It's great to see so many happy faces and feel the energy out there coming back at us. For in the final analysis, rock music is all about emotion, passion and connection. It's also about guitars!

My thanks to Pete Malandrone, Richard Gray, and Greg Brooks for supporting Simon all along the way, and to all my old friends who have kindly contributed their recollections to the text. Thanks also to Piers Murray Hill and the chaps at Carlton, who have carefully pushed me to the point where I couldn't possibly refuse to cooperate and get this thing out there on the shelves.

OK – before we begin – why the name 'Red Special'? It goes back a long way. In the early days, she was always just 'The Guitar', and I think it was Jock, one of my first guitar techs, who, in a moment of what one might call over-familiarity, likened his burden of taking care of it to taking care of a spouse, referring to my treasure as the 'Old Lady'. The appellation had an appeal, and kind of took root for a while. But, to me, this very personal instrument, with her humble beginnings in the minds and hands of my Dad and me, was worthy of a bit more respect than that. I remembered that at the time we finished the top coat of varnish, my Dad had wanted to christen her as the Brian May Special, and I had poo-pooed the idea; now I realised that it wasn't so uncool to give her a proper name. So one day in a radio interview, when someone asked me what I called the guitar, the words Red Special just tumbled out before I'd had time to think. And from then on, that was her name. There are now a few thousand Red Special replicas in the world, but my first love still keeps some of her mystery. She is, after all, a one-off!

Brian May, Las Vegas, July 2014

INTRODUCTION

As a guitar journalist and staunch Queen fan, I have always been flabbergasted that an official book detailing the construction of Brian May's Red Special didn't exist: it seemed a no-brainer, so I decided that I should tackle the somewhat daunting task of producing one myself.

I began working closely with Brian's Guitar Tech and right-hand man, my friend Pete Malandrone, to compile a list of contents that, with the help of a highly talented and dedicated team, has taken over three years to craft into this finished tome.

As much as I adore the music that the guitar had such a pivotal role in producing, I wanted the book to focus on the story of its conception, design and build, and put the reader right there in Harold May's workshop as the guitar took shape. What's more, I hoped that Brian would be the one to tell it.

Brian, playing the Red Special in the living room of the family home in Feltham, London, 1963.

There's more to the Red Special than the technical aspects, though; there's the human side too. The guitar represents a link to a part of Brian he's kept private up to now: the home-life of his earliest years, his relationship with his parents, specifically that with his father, and how that all dovetailed into the very genesis of Queen – and the birth of That Guitar.

For the book's centrepiece, Pete and I agreed early on that we'd take the hitherto unprecedented step of photographing an entirely dismantled Red Special for what would be the most intimate look at this iconic instrument there's ever been. The riskiness of the idea wasn't lost on anyone, but such is the trust that Brian had in us that he gave the go ahead: his expression as he first saw the pictures of his 'Old Lady' in pieces, a mixture of astonishment, fascination and horror, will stay with me for a long time.

Brian has been personally involved throughout the production process of this project, making time for a number of gruelling interviews, follow-up phone calls, emails and planning meetings. Perhaps most generously, he has also provided unrestricted access to his personal archives, and I'm very grateful for his guidance and unrelenting enthusiasm throughout.

Putting this book together has been a genuine pleasure, and I sincerely hope that the many thousands of others who have been similarly entranced by Queen and Brian May will enjoy poring over the myriad details of this world-famous guitar, as told by the man who's played it for more than half a century.

Simon Bradley (pictured left), Bath, February 2014

CHAPTER 1

FATHER TO SON

I asked Brian how it all began…

“I suppose I had a pretty sheltered childhood really; I was a typically shy only child. It was just my Mum, my Dad and me, and our cat. And whoever came into our world, like the neighbours and kids from school. But somewhere out there, in the dim and distant infinity, the birth of rock and roll was happening. My contact with it was listening to Radio Luxembourg on my crystal set radio (which my Dad had helped me make) whilst tucked up in bed pretending to be asleep. I still have the crystal set, together with its partner, a pair of German wartime earphones, apparently rescued from a submarine. When I look at these things I can still feel the thrill I got from lapping up those early Rock records – mainly from Pirate Radio stations.”

It was a very exciting time to be alive, and even though my world was very small, I was hugely aware of this catastrophic change that was going on in the world outside. It was already as if it were calling me… telling me what the central meaning of life for me would be. I used to go round to a friend's house regularly, at the tender age of around nine, and he had an older sister who was completely plugged into what was happening in the new rock and roll. That's where I first heard Little Richard – bursting out from her 45s played on a Dansette-type auto-changing record player (these words sound like they're from another world, now!) Little Richard blew my mind. I'd never heard raw passion in singing like that. I didn't know it was possible. And the beat was awesome… the pulse of anger, freedom, sex, all concepts I hardly understood yet, but sensed in this outrageous new music. As kids we were brought up with Frank Sinatra, Perry Como and Johnnie Ray on the radio in the background, and 'Music While You Work'; the noisiest it ever got was the big band stuff, Glenn Miller, Billy Cotton, but to hear this guy screaming – the whole dangerous energy of it – was just spell-binding. I remember thinking that this was the hard stuff – this was as raw and dirty as things could ever be. Actually, Little Richard's "Tutti Frutti" still gives me that feeling.

We had my dad's upright piano at home. He was very musical; he played by ear and could absorb anything. He could hear

Below: Ricky Nelson, circa 1958–59, with (right) guitarist James Burton, the latter sporting his Rickenbacker 381 prototype. Burton worked with Nelson from 1958 to 1966, and most famously performed with Elvis Presley.

anything on the radio and sit straight down and have a good stab at it on the piano, and I suppose that's kind of what I'm like. As a musician I'm instinctive, rather than one who can readily absorb music through dots – charts, sheet music. Again, like my Dad, I'm basically really bad at sight-reading, and that's what eventually put an end to my piano lessons; I took exams up to Grade 4 and then I couldn't bluff it any more! Interestingly, Freddie reached the same grade in piano at about the same time – but we didn't know each other in those days.

Strangely enough, not being a good reader of music doesn't really hold you back, at least not in the kind of world I've grown up in, because pretty much all the creative process is instinctive, and I've actually come to regard dots as a rather inadequate way of passing musical ideas on. You can get the bare bones, but charts don't transmit the feeling – the nuances that channel the passion that's in there. But if you're lucky enough to sit next to a guitar player (or any musician) while they're performing or composing, something special happens; that's the most incredibly direct transfer of knowledge for me. I've been privileged to do that with people like Hank Marvin, Rory Gallagher and Eric Clapton – heroes to me when I was a kid, and they still are. To be in a room with these guys and *feel* their work, see what their fingers are doing and the expression on their face, you can't help but absorb some real magic, and I guess that's the most precious thing.

My awakening to the guitar began with the ukulele. My Dad carried an instrument with him all throughout World War II, which people these days seem to call a Banjolele (he called it a ukulele-banjo) and he played in the style of George Formby. He'd sing and strum things like "When I'm Cleaning Windows" and "Chinese Laundry Blues", and I picked up the chords to these songs from my Dad quite easily. Then, hearing this new rock and roll stuff crashing in from the outside world, I made the connection; I could hear guitar music in my head and I wanted a guitar more than anything in the world.

So I asked my Mum and Dad for a guitar for what, I think, might have been my seventh birthday, and, bless them, they somehow managed to scrape together the seven guineas, or whatever it was, to buy me a guitar. When I woke up on my birthday there was this seemingly giant guitar on my bed,

Top: George Formby was a big influence on both Harold and Brian. "I have an original Formby ukulele that my Dad had with him all through the war and it's the one I used on Queen's 'Bring Back That Leroy Brown'."

Left: Jeff Beck influenced just about every English rock guitarist from the 1960s and 1970s thanks to his unique style. The young Brian was particularly enamoured by Beck's emotion and his control of feedback.

an Egmond, and it was amazing – pure magic. I can still smell the varnish!

Instantly, I started transferring chords from the ukulele and luckily it was in tune – I had no idea how to tune it! I realised the guitar had two extra strings down at the low end, so I had to figure out what to do with them. I did a lot of stuff with my thumb and worked the chords out for myself. Luckily enough I had friends who were doing the same thing, which helped.

I heard recently that George Harrison had an Egmond that was almost identical, and he always used to call it a crappy little guitar. Well, it's pretty basic, but to me it was the vehicle, my channel, towards being a guitarist and I'm still very fond of it.

Most of the new generation of singers I listened to at the time would strum the guitar (including Elvis and Cliff Richard), but standing next to them was the guy who was doing what I used to call the 'single notes': the lead guitarist. For a long time rhythm was all I could do and my whole apprenticeship was as an accompanist, which stood me in good stead, but I tried hard to work out how to play the single notes. In the middle of "Hello Mary Lou" by Ricky Nelson was – still is – this amazing solo, and to me the guitarist was talking; he was bending strings, as I discovered later, and making them sing with a passion – just like a vocalist. I didn't know then that this guy was James Burton, and he was one of the first in a generation of players who cut the guitar loose from its bonds. My mates and I had heard some sort of rumour that he did it by using banjo strings (rather than guitar strings) on his guitar, so off we went down to Clifford Essex, or BMG (Banjos, Mandolins and Guitars) in London just off Cambridge Circus. It was a lovely old-fashioned establishment and they would give you the banjo strings that had a little loop on the end, rather than the ball end you expected. The big thing was, of course, that they were thinner than any commercial guitar strings available at the time. And, in particular, it gave the guitar a plain steel third string, rather than the wire-wound third that all guitars seemed to come with in those days. We managed to get the strings on the guitar and they were light enough for us to be able to bend them – squeeze them sideways across the fingerboard, raising the pitch in an infinitely variable way – and that's where it all started for us. We would have been 13, 14 or 15 years old and we were drinking in everything that we could find.

On top of incisive guitar playing, Buddy Holly and The Crickets made that incredible harmony sound, which was like opening up a piece of the universe I'd never heard before. I felt emotions in my body I had no clue about: I just felt this incredible excitement and visceral pull, and I knew that was what I wanted to do. Buddy Holly did everything in just a

couple of years, but his output in that short time was incredible. I know The Crickets now, I'm lucky enough to have met and worked with them, but I think even they found it difficult to quantify the magic that happened; I suppose it's like me looking back on "Keep Yourself Alive" (Queen's very first single). I asked them how it all happened, how they did "Maybe Baby" and "Oh Boy!", and they were like: "Well, we just went in there, set up the bass..."! To me, whatever it was that happened in those sessions is utterly and eternally magical: it spooks me still. A lot of early Queen music comes from stuff like that, from those kinds of feelings, and I know The Beatles felt this same way about Buddy Holly – a total hero – a groundbreaker.

I also remember a little later hearing "Quarter To Three" by Gary U.S. Bonds. Now they call that Rhythm and Blues, though this phrase meant something a little different to us – something related to Chuck Berry and Lightnin' Hopkins – also great groundbreaking artists and influences on us. In "Quarter To Three" the guy's almost not singing, he's almost shouting, and the backing is all claps and stamps... sound familiar? That was pretty raw – and still is

Listening to Buddy Holly and Little Richard for the first time was just colossal for me and it seemed that America was where it all was happening, and, at that time, of course that was very much true. Of course, things later changed vastly, and there was this two-way traffic of inspiration across the Atlantic, of which we became a part. The Beatles changed everything – opened the doors – and let loose an explosion.

Lonnie Donegan was a big thing for me too, and he was essentially home-grown, but heavily influenced by American Blues, and he was really the first guy to bring a hint of that earthy reality of the Blues to Britain. Lonnie was hard rockin' long before the golden age of Eric Clapton and the big influx of blues music that happened later. He was influenced by Leadbelly, amongst others, and he brought in that kind of 'speaking from the heart',

Opposite Top: Jimi Hendrix, an unquestionable genius of the electric guitar. Like many others, Brian wondered just how Jimi did what he did...

Opposite Below: Bluesman Rory Gallagher, who, by introducing Brian to the tonal wonders of the Vox AC30, inadvertently spawned a legend.

Below: An advertisement for Vox amplifiers from the mid-1960s, showing the AC30 alongside an AC50 head and 2x12 cabinet array most famously used by The Beatles, and echo and reverb units "...for way-out sounds."

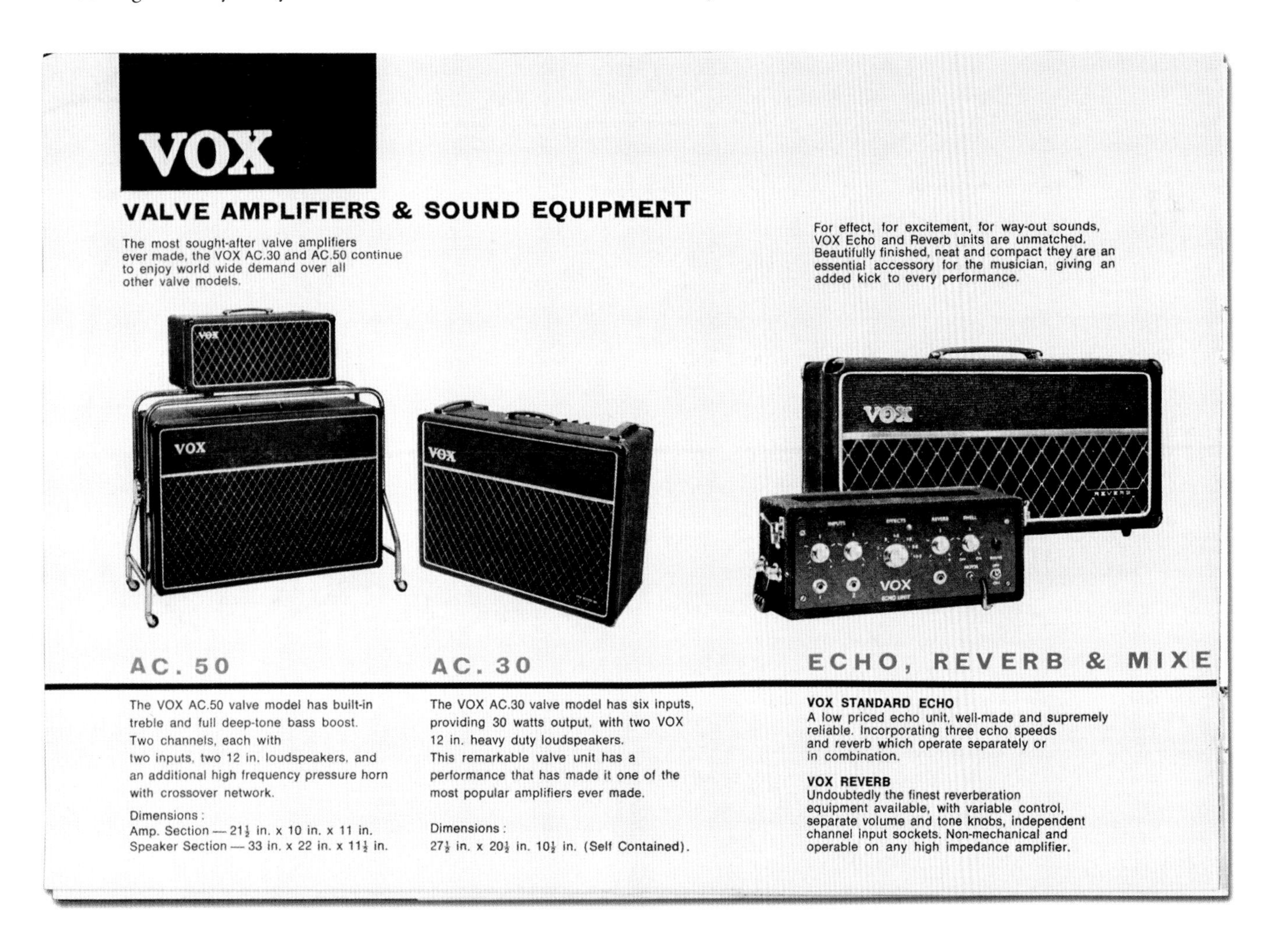

singing about the pain you have inside: I was hugely moved by that. I also liked his humour and was conscious that he embraced a bit of English culture too: "My Old Man's A Dustman" is pure English Music Hall, updated to the Skiffle genre, which Lonnie pretty much invented. Skiffle had a big motivating effect on us kids, because you could make it yourselves just with simple gear – acoustic guitars, washboards, tea chest bass and vocals. Around that time I also fell in love with Connie Francis and a whole era of passionate, emotive pop. To me, *our* music was built on naked emotion. That's why it engulfed and electrified us.

Suddenly guitars were amplified. In the beginning, pickups were put on guitars so they could be heard amongst a band, without the problems of feedback associated with putting a guitar in front of a live microphone. Les Paul was one of the pioneers of the amplified guitar, and his recordings are a fascinating legacy of invention; but once you amplify a guitar, you change its character, and the more you amplify, the more its character changes. The first thing to happen is that it starts to sustain in a very nice way, which extends its ability to be a voice. It's louder too, but if you start driving the amplifier hard, it compresses the signal, and the guitar *really* starts to sing. An old-style valve (tube) amplifier driven into distortion changes the whole nature of a single note into something more akin to a saxophone or violin. And what it does to chords is... something else! It sounds... angry! Metal could never have become Heavy without overdriven tube amplifiers!

So the first time I heard the English bluesmen, guys like Clapton and Jeff Beck, they'd figured it all out from the American Blues players, the guys who had it in their souls. I don't know who told Howling Wolf to plug his guitar into an amplifier, but it suddenly became this dirty, passionate instrument that was able to get emotion across like a powerful voice. I used to go into record shops and look for any guitar music whatsoever – Charlie Bird, Chet Atkins, Django Reinhardt – it was all inspiring.

Above: Lazing on a Sunday afternoon, Harold, Ruth and Brian May enjoy some quality family time by the sea, circa 1950.

Right: Brian's first guitar, a small-bodied Egmond acoustic that he received on his seventh birthday, in 1954. It's still in surprisingly good condition.

But I was drawn, by that journey, into distortion, a kind of ripping sound. Clapton got a Gibson Les Paul and plugged into a Marshall that, in those days, I'm sure was always turned up full. It sang, it screamed, it was just the bee's knees. Clapton was God. I was massively inspired by all that: I was a kid, but I felt I was in tune with everything. I loved the Beatles too, of course, and interestingly George Harrison didn't use a lot of that sustain or distortion, at least not until later, but he just had such a great creative mind and technique that it didn't matter.

Then… there was Hendrix. Jimi Hendrix was the pinnacle of this whole thing, of course. He was working with the distortion, sustain and feedback and he took the guitar to a whole other level. He somehow managed to make the guitar give out more than he was putting in. It was *alive*. Jimi was somehow gathering energy from the ether, and the guitar became almost uncontrollable: he was holding it back the whole time. It really was a kind of miracle.

I first went to see him live at the Saville Theatre, promoted by The Beatles manaer Brian Epstein *[The Jimi Hendrix Experience last played the London theatre on August 27, 1967 – SB]*. I'd heard the record "Hey Joe", with a beautifully mellow solo, but when you turned the disc over, there was the manic "Stone Free", where the guitar sounds like it has a mind of its own, and Jimi was talking to the guitar, and it was talking back! I guess I didn't think that it could be real, that it must have been some sort of studio technique or something, but I saw him and suddenly he was doing it all in front of me and all the other unbelievers, who soon became disciples. Hendrix could do that live, and it was dazzling and life-changing for me. I think everyone was blown away by Hendrix and that was the moment where I thought I either had to give it up because it was too scary, or else I had to devote myself to finding out whatever it was that Jimi was immersed in. So I plunged in.

Hendrix on stage was all about his passion, his guitar and the amplifier, and his sound had a special sort of wonderfully smooth, almost orchestral, distortion. I wondered how he did that, and the answer was actually given to me by Rory Gallagher. We used to go and see him every Thursday night at the Marquee and the boys and I would sneak into the back rooms when everyone was leaving so we'd be able to see him after the gig. He'd come out and pack up his own gear, and we'd ask him how he did it. He was the nicest, most patient guy you could imagine – a real gentleman – and he told me about his guitar and a little box called a Dallas Rangemaster treble booster. He showed me his amps and he said he used the Vox amps because "…they just speak…"

So a bunch of us went straight down Tottenham Court Road to a second hand amp shop called, I think, Take 5, and they had a few

Above: Summer, 1954. Harold May turns his considerable musical talents to the guitar. “He was very musical,” says Brian. “He could absorb anything.”

Below: Brian, at home, playing his beloved acoustic, the guitar that drove Brian to create the Red Special, complete with a few Egmond-inspired features, 1954.

Vox AC30s, all beaten up, with torn coverings, and all in a row. I plugged my guitar, my Red Special, through a Rangemaster box that I'd meanwhile found, into one of these amps and the sound was just *there*. It sang, it had that throaty depth, the overtones, the sustain, and the 'splutter' that I was searching for, and I was just ... well, it was like a religious experience! I just knew that that was the sound I'd always been looking for – my voice – so I bought two at £25 each, which was a big investment, took them home and that was it. That's still it: I don't use anything between the amp and the guitar except for a little treble booster that we make ourselves now – all treble boosters are modelled on that old Rangemaster circuit, no matter what they tell you! That was my voice, and it's never changed from that time: it just does it right.

So... the Guitar!

Of course we're darting back and forth in time here, but we made my Red Special, my Dad and I, in my Dad's workshop – converted from the spare bedroom in our small suburban house in Feltham, Middlesex – in about two years of spare moments, and it was all done with hand tools – planes, chisels and saws, and a lot of sandpaper, fashioning the thing out of bits and pieces. For the neck, we used part of an old fireplace that at the time was 100 years old; it was just kicking around the workshop. If you look really closely, you can still see wormholes that I filled up with matchsticks. My Dad had all kinds of stuff that he'd made, things like test instruments for radios and TVs, and he had the tools as well. He had lots of stock he thought might be useful one day and if we wanted something for the guitar, we could normally find it in a corner of the workshop.

So, for two years or so, we'd come up to the workshop and work away on the guitar, all by hand, and some of the time it was quite tough. The centre part of the body was made from a piece of oak table, hard like steel, and to fashion that took endless hours of work: it blunted all of our tools and gave us blisters on our hands!

My Dad really was a great Dad, and he was helpful with anything I wanted to do. Any passion that I had, he'd back me up and get into it. I know he enjoyed building the guitar very much and I don't think we ever fell out over it. He used to fall out with himself from time to time and I remember him slipping with a chisel and making a big gouge on the body; he just couldn't forgive himself. My Dad's old hammer is also a big thing for me, still to this day. There was something about his hands, his bony hands, holding this hammer; that image I have of him sums him up in my mind and that old hammer of his means so much to me.

A lot of swearing went on, but eventually we got there. Quite often we would slip up and something would go wrong, and we'd think the whole thing was ruined. But we'd find some way around it and repair it.

Above: Brian takes a break from his studies to strum an acoustic owned by Dave Dilloway, who went on to play bass in Brian's first band, 1984.

Left: Dave Dilloway's acoustic guitar, now owned by Brian, in detail. Dave sadly passed away in 2011.

Top and Middle: The 16-year-old Brian indulging his Beatles fantasies with his Egmond acoustic (*See* p17) in the May family home, October 1963.

Above: The Red Special makes its first-ever public appearance, at the Molesey Boat Club in Putney, 1966, with Brian's first band 1984. Note the original pickups that would soon be replaced with three Burns Tri-Sonics.

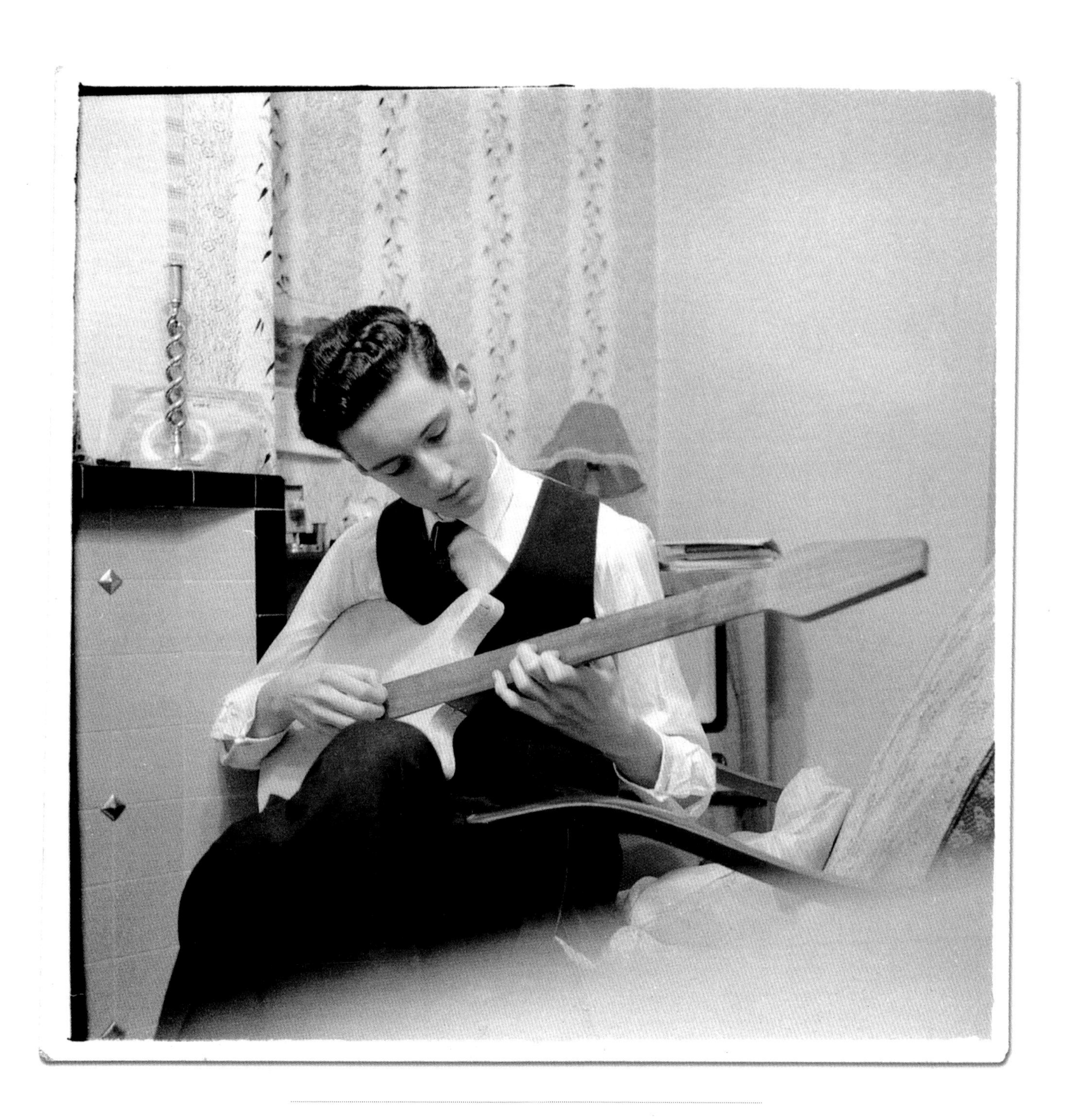

Above: A wonderful shot from May 1963 that sees Brian in a world of his own with the Red Special, imagining what it will become. At this stage, the guitar had neither fingerboard nor any electrics, and is yet to be stained.

It was character-forming. Building this thing became our lives for two years and you had to learn to forgive yourself as well as try to achieve perfection. Lots of important life lessons there! Being a perfectionist is fine, but it can really kill you, and, much later and on a broader scale, I learned that perfectionism is quite evil and can destroy you – it can lead to addictive behaviours, depressions and whatever.

Dad and I got on very well during this period and it's odd, because the trouble happened later. At that time I was at school, then went on to University and studied Physics, Maths and Astronomy, and went all the way into the PhD. I did four years of a PhD in Astronomy, which is what Astrophysics was called back then. I was pursuing the kind of life that my Dad imagined I was destined for – something academic – and the guitar was just a great hobby.

The first public engagement I played at was with 1984, my first group with my pal, the late Dave Dilloway; it was at the Molesey Boat Club in Putney. I had made the guitar by then, and it still had the old original home-made pickups in it at that point. I used to play things like "Happy Hendrik's Polka" by The Spotnicks, which was really hard to get my fingers around – I could only just do it – and we played it at that gig. There's a recording of it somewhere, and you can hear someone exclaiming "Oooh, look at 'is fingers move!" – so that was my first good review, I guess! We also used to do covers of Motown songs, things like "Knock On Wood" and "My Girl", and a little bit of Cream and Hendrix too. So that was my first gig and we went on to do a few small shows as a semi-pro outfit. We used to make about £20 a gig, which was respectable in those days, but by the time you'd paid somebody's petrol to drive you, you'd go home with thirty bob [one pound ten shillings – a pound and a half!], or sometimes nothing.

1984 disintegrated once I went to college, but Tim Staffell – the singer – kept in touch, and we formed this group called Smile. That's another story. Later, when we'd already started in with Queen, Smile's successor, I had to make the decision whether to carry on

Below: 1984, eyeing the high life. Once the band fell apart, Brian went on to form Smile with singer Tim Staffell (far right).

Left: Tim Staffell is stood in front of Brian's amp, possibly leading to the difficulty he's displaying here in hearing himself sing.

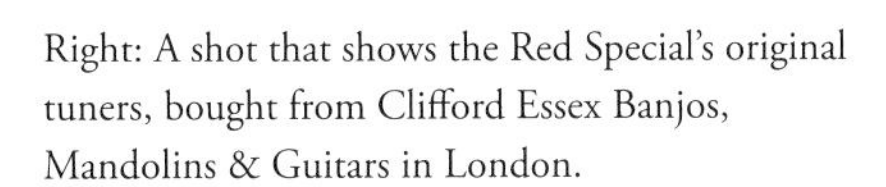

Right: A shot that shows the Red Special's original tuners, bought from Clifford Essex Banjos, Mandolins & Guitars in London.

Left: The full 1984 live experience, with Brian and the Red Special far left. We can clearly see his Burns Orbit amp too, perched on a stool behind the band, at head height for improved projection.

with the PhD and finish it off, or go out and step into the void.

We obviously had no idea what the hell would happen if we *did* step into the void, and that first Mott The Hoople tour *[Queen's first show supporting Mott was at Leeds Town Hall, November 12, 1973 – SB]* was the first time we seriously became a working group. We'd done odd bits and pieces before, but this was like 'pack your bags'. We left home, went out and stayed in crap hotels because we were poor. We shared rooms, slept in the van if we had to, and just became working, travelling musicians.

My Dad just could not compute it. He said: "You've got this far, you have all this education…" and, of course, he'd sacrificed a lot of his life to get me my education; he'd worked so hard just to get me through university. He just couldn't believe that I was chucking it all away and going out to be a pop star… or a failure!

So, that was hard, and our relationship became very strained, but I remember saying to him at the times when we did speak, "Dad, you helped me make the guitar, you're a part of this, but you're so against me going through with it." And he said; "But you're throwing away your career – your life" It was really tough, and my Mum was caught in the middle. She had a terrible time and had what in those days was called a nervous breakdown because she was trying to stay close to both of us, but it wasn't possible because we were diametrically opposed. She was actually taken away to hospital in a terrible state of collapse so finally both my Dad and I realised what we were doing and how destructive it was. So we kind of got back together and came to an understanding, which was cemented when Queen went to America and played Madison Square Garden for the first time. *[Queen first played the legendary New York venue on February 5, 1977 and are part of an elite group of artists to sell out two nights there – which they did on December*

Above: Ruth and Harold May, backstage at New York's Madison Square Garden after witnessing Brian and Queen perform a "mind-blowing" show. The joy, as father and son reconnect, is obvious from their expressions.

1 and 2, 1977.] We still didn't have much money and I flew my Mum and Dad out on Concorde – he had worked on Concorde's blind landing system as a radar engineer, but had never been able to afford to fly on it.

They came out with my new wife and my newly-born son Jimmy, and I put them all up at The Ritz, and said: "Order room service, Dad; we're rich!" Of course, we weren't, but he was touched that I'd done that and was happy to be a part of it, although I now think he probably felt very out of place, and uncomfortable.

My parents came to the show, actually sat in with the audience. I will never forget that night; the response we got from that audience was just mind-blowing. My Dad wasn't a physical, huggy kind of person, but he came back afterwards, shook my hand and said: "OK – I get it. Now I see what you are doing, and why it is so important to you". That was a big moment for me as it swept away all the problems that we'd had and, from that point on, he was unreservedly into the music. I think secretly he always had been, but now, being a musician, he was able to give himself over to it and enjoy it, and that was a godsend for me. You can be a rebel, and we all do it – kick against our upbringing – but in the end, no matter far you've wandered off the rails, you always want your parents' approval.

All the time we were touring, Dad was making little maps back home and putting lines on them, showing our progress, constructing graphs of our chart positions – getting into it, in his own way. He just had a problem seeing music as a real job. We'd talk about it in a more understanding way later on, and joke about it. I'd say: "Well, I never did get a proper job, did I, Dad?"

And, truly, I never did.

Above: Parts that would become the Red Special, August 1963. "The strange device to the left of the pickups is something I bought at one of the second-hand shops in London," says Brian. "It's probably some kind of mount for something in a submarine, but I put bullraces and a stainless steel tube in it, which was our original design for a low friction tremolo."

Queen
Tour
April/May 1978
START
FINISH
27/9
STUTTGART
MUNICH
16/9
MILAN
14,15/9
Queen
July -
MILWAUKEE
CHICAGO
INDIANAPO
CINCINNATI
MPHIS
QUEEN
30/1
GLASGOW
NEWCASTLE
3,4
LIVERPOOL
6,7
26,27
MANCHESTER
DUBLIN
22
24
BIRMINGHAM
CORK
13 to 26
LONDON
9
BRISTOL
10,11
BRIGHTON
QUEEN CRA
Tuesday 20 NOVEMBER
Thursday 22 NOVEMBER
Saturday 24 NOVEMBER
Monday 26 NOVEMBER
Tuesday 27 NOVEMBER
Friday 30 NOVEMBER
Saturday 1 DECEMBER
Monday 3 DECEMBER
Tuesday 4 DECEMBER
Thursday 6 DECEMBER
Friday 7 DECEMBER
Sunday 9 DECEMBER
Monday 10 DECEMBER
Tuesday 11 DECEMBER
CRAZY TOUR
Thursday 13 DECEMBER
Friday 14 DECEMBER
Monday 17 DECEMBE
Wednesday 19 DECEMBE
Thursday 20 DECEMBE
Saturday 22 DECEMBE
Wednesday 26 DECEMBE
Vancouver
GLASGOW
30-31,15
CANADA
USA

BRAZIL
HOME
RIO DE JANEIRO 17, 18,
SÃO PAULO
20
PORTO ALEGRE 13
ARGENTINA
ROSARIO 6
BUENOS AIRES 28, 1, 8
MAR DEL PLATA
22 Los Angeles
Long Beach 20/21
San Diego 16
15
Pacific Ocean
14 VANCOUVER
UR'79
Hall
AM N.E.C.
TER Apollo
TER Apollo
V Apollo
V Apollo
TLE City Hall
TLE City Hall
L Empire
L Empire
Hippodrome
N Centre
N Centre
DON
EUM
NBOW
'S, Purley
R, Tottenham
, Lewisham
NDRA PALACE
RSMITH Odeon
American Tour '78
Key Date
OCT.
1 28 Dallas
2 29 Memphis
3 31 New Orleans
NOV.
4 3 Miami
5 4 Lakeland
6 6 Washington DC
7 7 New Haven
8 9 Detroit
10 Detroit
9 11 Kalamazoo
10 13 Boston
14 Boston
11 16 New York
17 New York
12 19 Nassau
13 20 Philadelphia
14 22 Nashville
15 23 St.Louis
16 25 Cleveland
17 26 Cincinnati
18 28 Buffalo
19 30 Ottawa
Key Date
DEC.
20 1 Montreal
21 3 Toronto
4 Toronto
22 6 Madison
23 7 Chicago
24 8 Kansas City
25 12 Seattle
26 13 Portland
27 14 Vancouver
28 16 San Francisco
29 18 Los Angeles
19 Los Angeles
20 Los Angeles
→en-route-HOME
18/19/20 LOS ANGE
CAGO
17 INDIANAPOLIS
LEVE

BUZZER
LAMP
MAN
OFF
ON

CHAPTER 2

A GUITAR IS BORN

So let's get down to business! When was the moment that Brian and his father decided to construct their own instrument?

“We were talking about the old Egmond acoustic guitar. I still have it, and it's been through the wars over the years; my mate took all the finish off it and drilled holes in it to make it do various things, but I recently had it restored to pretty much how it looked on that birthday morning, gleaming like a toffee apple. It was nice and easy to play, with a low action, and early on I worked out that if you put your hand on the tailpiece and wiggled it, you could get a sort of tremolo effect.”

But I now wanted that guitar to be electric. Dad was an electronics engineer – his special field of expertise during the War was Radar and Radio – and although he didn't know anything about guitars, he knew a whole lot about amplifiers, which was to become very useful.

I was thinking about electric guitar pickups, and I figured out that there must be some way that the steel string perturbed the magnetic field of these magnets that had a coil around them, and this generated an electric current which varied as the string moved, producing that special signal – the information which was to be amplified. What an amazingly exciting thought! So I bought some Eclipse button magnets from this hardware shop in Kingston upon Thames that I used to visit most Saturday mornings in those days, and set to work making my own pickup. Of course there had to be thousands of windings to generate enough signal from those tiny magnetic variations, so the coil had to be made of very fine copper wire. But getting that hair-thin wire on there was tricky because it broke so easily. Dad, who was great at making all kinds of things, improvised a great low-stress pickup winding device, which, again, I still have. It had a revolution counter – a mileometer borrowed from a bicycle – so you knew exactly how many turns were on there. I used that winder to make all my home-made pickups. So, there it was! Three magnets in a line in the pickup, and thousands of turns of wire wrapped around them. There was a magic moment when I first connected the two ends of the wire to an input of our radio – made by Dad, of course. He'd made our TV, our radio, our record player, and a high quality tape recorder, and he had this lovely amplifier that had 'co-ax' inputs. So I slid the pickup under the strings on the guitar, and plugged the device into my Dad's amp, and – glory be – it worked! I think it probably drove the neighbours mad, but it made this very good sound, sort of bright and zingy – like nothing I'd ever heard before. It was alive. My old guitar was electrified!

The pickup had one problem, though. When you bent the string, which of course I wanted to do, there was a strange 'fsh-fsh' noise as it moved across the pickup, and I figured out that it must have been because the magnets were lined up so their polarities were North/South, North/South rather than all North. I planned to cut the magnets in half, and put all the North poles in a line, but I didn't have the tools to do that… and it never happened.

Because I was so comfortable with the old guitar, I very much

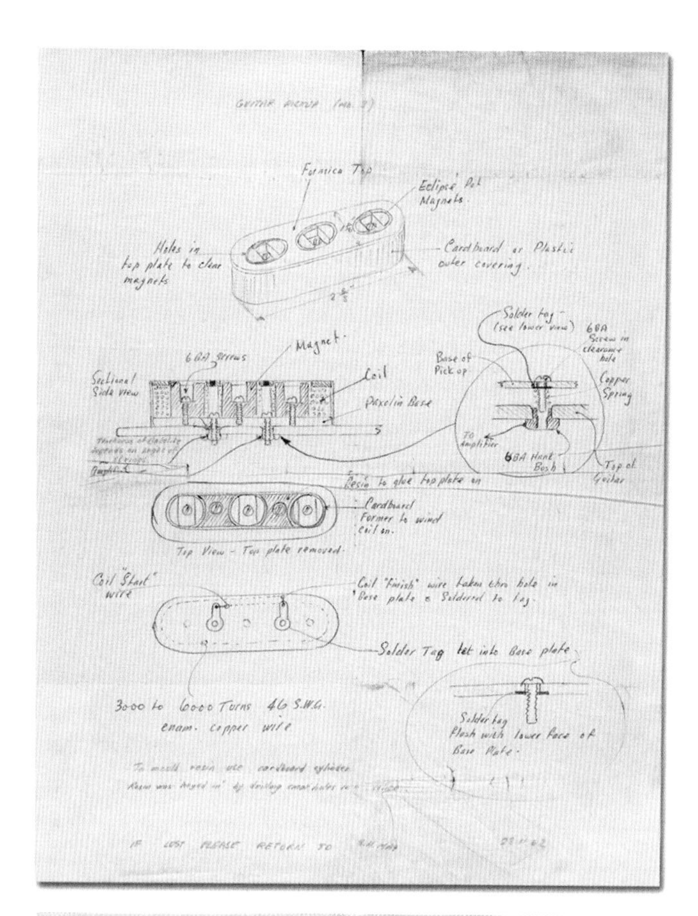

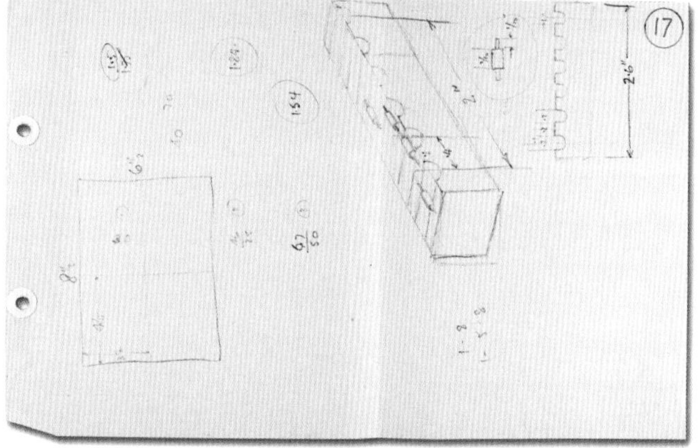

Top and Above: Two fascinating hand-drawn documents from Brian's personal archives. The top one, dated November 28, 1962, shows the design of the first pickups fitted to the Red Special, while the other features the dimensions of the aluminium bridge and roller saddles.

Left: The original pickup Brian made to electrify his Egmond acoustic, using Eclipse magnets and tested through an amplifier made by Harold. The first pickups fitted to the Red Special followed the same principles.

Right: A detailed and intricate diagram of the neck joint, showing the truss rod bolt and the curve of the heel. "I gradually whittled it away until it felt good and I was roughly aiming for the profile of my old acoustic's neck."

Overleaf: Just part of a detailed description of the processes involved in building the Red Special, as written by Brian soon after the guitar had been finished.

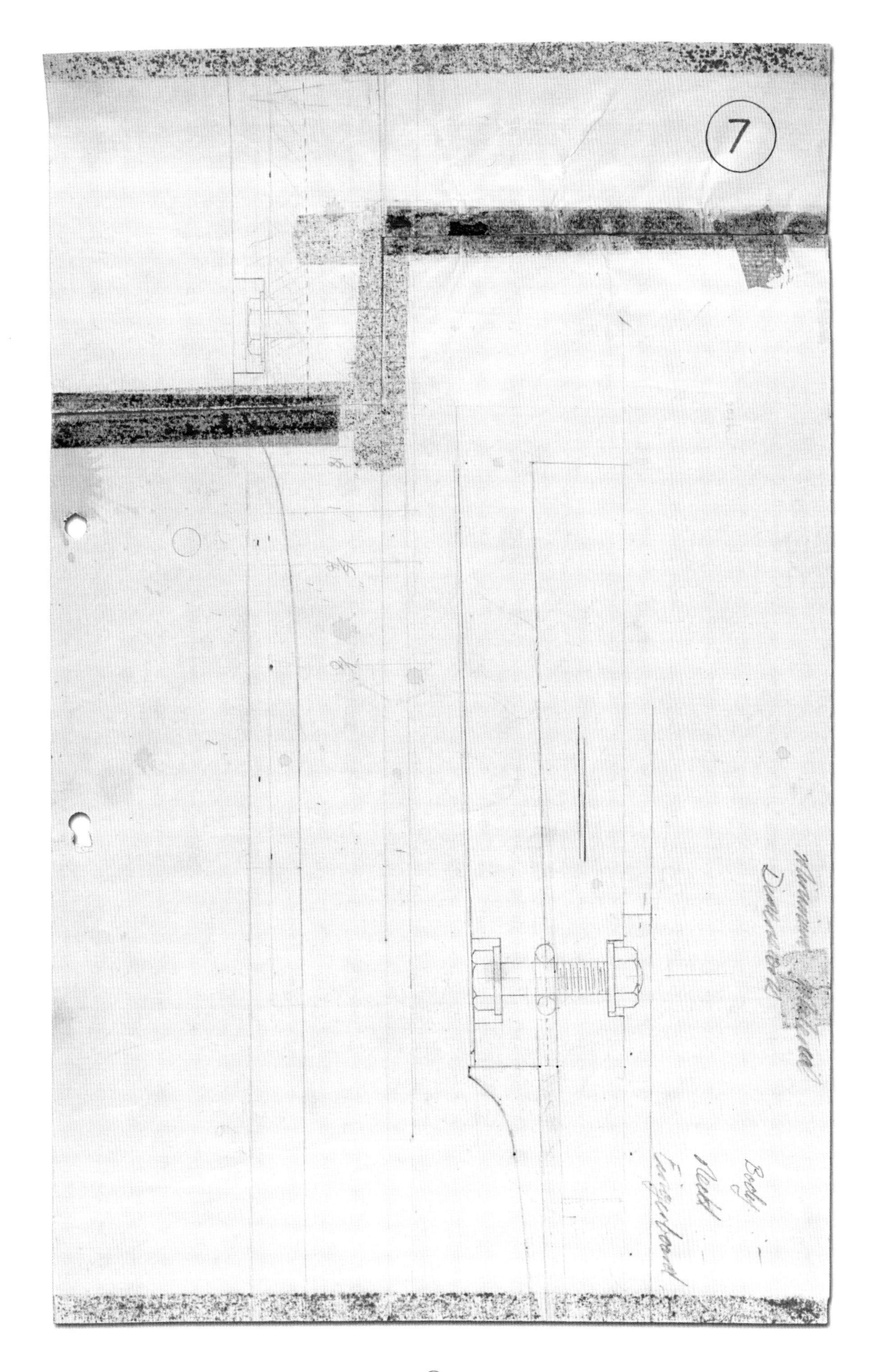
7
Body
Neck
Fingerboard

A. EXTERNAL BODY SHAPING.

A rough idea of the maximum dimensions of the body were decided. A number of sheets of greaseproof paper were Sellotaped together and the outline was drawn full size on these sheets in pencil.

With carbon paper the tracing was transferred to the material to be used in two places (since the body was to be double-thickness) and inked in. The strips of the blockboard were made parallel to the neck. The two laminae were cut out with a fret-saw in conjunction with a supply of blades. That part fastening the neck in place was provisionally cut straight across, leaving a wide margin for the fitting process.

The two halves were screwed together so that their edges corresponded as closely as possible. The composite edge was more finely shaped by:-

1. Planing with the work protruding over the edge of the table, a method found to be less useful than:-

2. Chiselling, with the work placed flat on a hard surface, the chisel being pushed downwards until it hit the surface.

3. Sandpapering. This was done, again by putting the work flat on a hard surface, and using a piece of sandpaper fastened round a cylindrical former. The base of the cylinder was kept pressed against the surface of the bench, so the edge was maintained perpendicular.

The part where the neck was to join was left untouched.

6. EXTERNAL NECK SHAPING

The vertical projection of the neck was transferred to the top of the wood in a similar way to the body, taking care to allow enough length for the inclined extreme end of the head. The outline was roughly cut with a tenon saw.

The edges of the actual neck were planed straight, and the straight edges of the head were similarly treated, but the corners were left on for the time being.

The horizontal projection, or elevation, was drawn on the edges.

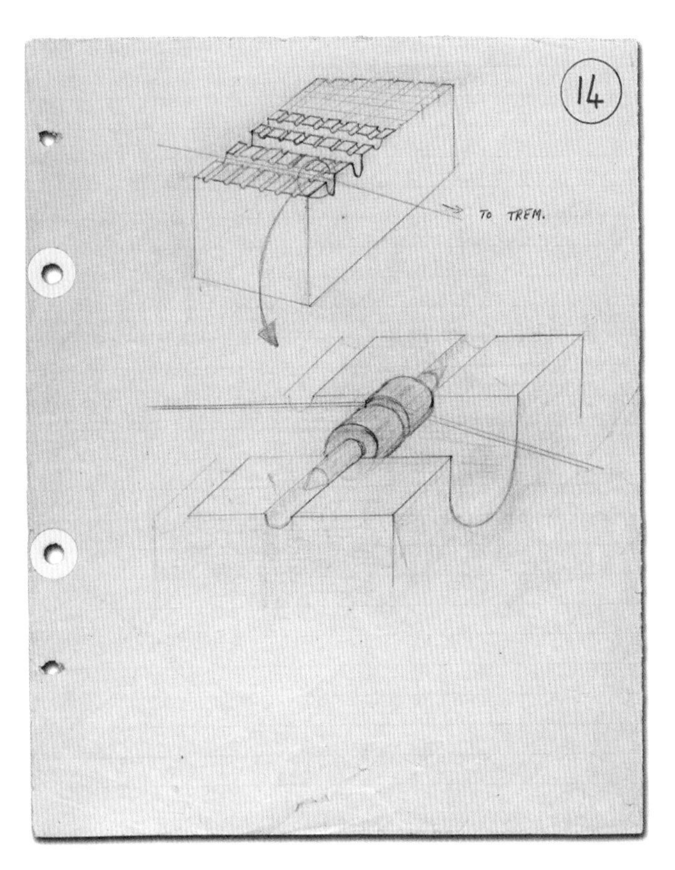

fret	24		27	24·5
	B	N	N	
1	22·6531	1·3469	1·5153	1·3745
2	21·3809	2·6191	2·9465	
3	20·1802	3·8198	4·2969	
4	19·04902	4·9510	5·5696	
5	17·9793	6·0207	6·7731	
6	16·9697	7·0303	7·9089	
7	16·0167	7·9833	8·9807	
8	15·1211	8·8789	9·9881	
9	14·2719	9·7281	10·9438	
10	13·4704	10·5298	11·8456	
11	12·7140	11·2860	12·6962	
12	12·0000	12·0000	13·5000	
13	11·3268	12·6732	14·2569	
14	10·6907	13·3093	14·9727	
15	10·0903	13·9097	15·6481	
16	9·5236	14·4764	16·2854	
17	8·9889	15·0111	16·8874	
18	8·4841	15·5159	17·4551	
19	8·0077	15·9923	17·9908	
20	7·5580	16·4420	18·4970	
21	7·1335	16·8665	18·9743	
22	6·7339	17·2671	19·4138	
23	6·3569	17·6430	19·8481	
24	6·0000	18·0000	20·2500	18·368

Ref. 3662

used it as a model for how I wanted the electric to feel, with quite a thick neck and a low fret profile. Now, developing my 'single notes' technique, I tended to get lost as I worked my way further up towards the 'dusty end' of the fingerboard, so I decided I needed to add another position dot to the Egmond fingerboard. I added the extra dot at the seventh fret, fashioned from a button from my mum's sewing box. It was real mother of pearl, and I marked it all out and carefully filed it into shape. To get it perfectly round, I made a template – a steel rod, to stick it on and do the final filing and polishing. The template came in very useful when I came to making *all* the dots for the new Red Special, which was a much bigger task! I know each dot personally. They're all slightly different; unique patterns and colours appear in the mother of pearl. So again, it all started with wanting to adapt my first guitar.

The pickup worked pretty well on the Egmond, apart from the string-bending problem, but it was plain that we needed to go further. I wanted a full electric instrument with multiple pickups and a proper tremolo, and something which would feed back in the 'right' way, enhancing the sustain. I had big ideas! I couldn't afford to buy an electric guitar – there was no way; I couldn't even afford a copy of the Fenders and Gibsons that looked so enticing in the brochures. So my Dad and I decided we would make one.

We did actually sit down and design it, and I wanted it to look like an acoustic guitar that had been cut away: it's my own shape. I started with something that was more or less the Egmond shape and then did my own cutaways. I decided on two cutaways because I genuinely wanted to get up to the top end of the fingerboard. I also couldn't see why most electrics stopped at the 22nd fret – just short of two octaves. Why not have the full two? So the guitar was designed with a fingerboard that went up to the 24th fret.

So, it was all mapped out, all designed, and then we just worked and worked on it, with some experimentation thrown in, for about two years. All of the hardware and electrics were designed from scratch because there were no such things as tremolos and tremolo-friendly bridges in those days; there were just loose screws! I wanted to make sure that if the tremolo was used even to extremes, the strings would return to the correct pitch. The Fender Synchronized tremolo system was essentially just some screws that aren't fully screwed in and the bridge piece thing wobbled about. I realised that the reason an instrument would not return properly to pitch was friction. Friction would stop the string equalising out the tension in its various parts along its length – a kind of 'hysteresis'.

Above Left: A beautifully rendered pencil drawing of a roller saddle and how it fits into its own aluminium bridge block. As the vibrato arm is depressed, the string moves forward and the rollers ensure they return perfectly in tune.

Above Right: The exact measurements – to four decimal places – of the distance of the frets from the bridge and nut in a 24-inch scale. 'B' refers to bridge, 'N' to nut and 24, 27 and 24.5 to the scale length.

Friction had to be eliminated as far as possible if the guitar was going to stay in tune after the tremolo was used. We came up with various tremolo devices, one of which was a tubular design on ball bearings, but then we had the idea of setting a bridge-piece of mild steel rocking on a knife-edge. I think somebody somewhere had a similar idea at the same moment, but for us it was a completely new solution to our problem. And it really worked. We managed to make an almost frictionless tremolo, but it needed a bridge that was frictionless too, otherwise the instrument wouldn't stay in tune. Again, I made some designs and worked on them until we had it figured out.

The bridge was sawn and filed out from one block of aluminium. My idea was to use tiny stainless steel rollers instead of saddles for the strings to go over at the tremolo end, so again there was almost no friction. I was able to file out all the slots for the rollers in one go and then cut it up into the six pieces. The little rollers were pretty hard to make, of course, as I didn't have a lathe. So, improvising as normal, I put a manual drill into a vice, put the little piece of steel rod into the drill, turned it and it became a sort of hand-made, hand-powered lathe that worked against the file I had in my other hand. Of course, if you went too far it would go 'plink' – break – and you'd have wasted the whole three hours it had taken you to get that far ! I had to learn fast!

Later, when the guitar was in use, every time I broke a string there was a risk of the roller disappearing, since they're not captive within the bridge – they're genuinely free-running. So, unless we were lucky and could see it roll across the stage, we had to have a supply of spares. I used to make them all myself but we eventually found somebody who could make rollers for us, which was very useful. Some later roller bridges inspired by our invention did in fact make the rollers captive, but I never did. One reason was connected with the way I play, which is always with the heel of my right hand on the bridge. It gives me more control over the sound… I can do a kind of 'half-mute', which thickens the sound of those 'single notes'.

Actually, there are quite a few innovations on the guitar. The roller bridge was, I think, unique in those days and everybody was saying I should have patented it, but patents are a pain in the neck, and why not share everything with the world? A fingerboard with 24 frets was unusual, so I introduced an extension of the marker dots to save me from getting lost. Instead of two dots at the 12th fret I put three – so the twos could go elsewhere. The truss rod was anchored on a massive bolt which also fastens the neck on to the body… so tightening it up really held the neck rigid. The tremolo uses compression springs (borrowed from a British Norton Motorbike – they're valve springs) rather than springs in tension like most other term units. And, unusually for the time, it sat completely in equilibrium in the centre position, so I could rock the pitch smoothly either way. Also I devised my own system for switching between combinations of the three pickups, so, for the first time I think, *all* the possible combinations of three pickups, in and out of phase, could be used in preformance. There are a few other things, like the acoustic pocket in the body, which

Below: The home-made pickup winder with which Brian hand-wound his first guitar pickups. A true artefact that has remained in his possession.

I'll mention again in a moment. It also has a slightly shorter scale length (effective string length) than most commercial guitars, making the fingering a little easier, and the tone a little brighter.

The guitar originally had three pickups almost exactly like the one I made for the Egmond. They were a little bit narrower, as there wasn't much room. For each one, the three Eclipse button magnets were mounted in a line on a plastic base, covered with a thin plastic former for the coil. On this went a few thousand turns of copper wire – 48 or 50 gauge, I seem to remember, wound with that home-made coil winder. The copper wire coil was then covered with white cloth tape. The ends of the coil were terminated in contacts on the underside of the base – metal washers through which the screws went to hold the pickup on to the body of the guitar. The screws located into nuts embedded in the wood of the guitar, and these were connected to the switching array though wires also embedded in the wood. So attaching the pickup also made the contact for the pickups to be in circuit, with no loose wires; it was a good system. I'd plug into my Dad's home-made radio by way of the input circuits on the preamp for our Collaro three-speed tape deck, and out came that magic electric sound. The pickups had a wonderful bright tone. They sounded very smooth, with a nice bright sound; I still have some tape recordings of me playing direct into the tape recorder in those early days, and it's something unusual.

But the same thing happened that had happened with the Egmond – the polarity problem that I still don't fully understand, which threatened to stop me bending strings. Not good enough!

So that's what eventually sent me down to the Burns shop to buy some pickups. Their shop, at that time, was underneath the new Centre Point building at Tottenham Court Road, so close to the Dominion Theatre where, much later, *We Will Rock You* was to root itself for 12 years. They didn't have much choice: the only Burns pickups they had for sale loose were, of course, Tri-Sonics. They were three guineas each and I bought three of them, wrapped in tissue paper. They did the trick, and they are the same pickups that are still there today.

An interesting story about the frets. I was fascinated by the idea of why frets were set at particular distances: why did they get narrower towards the body? I figured out that what happens is reproducible. If you want to convert the string length that produces a certain note to the length that makes a note a semitone higher, there must be a certain proportional change in string length. In other words, to get one semitone higher, there must be some factor (less than 1) that would multiply the string length by, to get that semitone. So, if you call that proportional factor 'x', you multiply the total string length by 'x' and you get the distance from the bridge to the fret

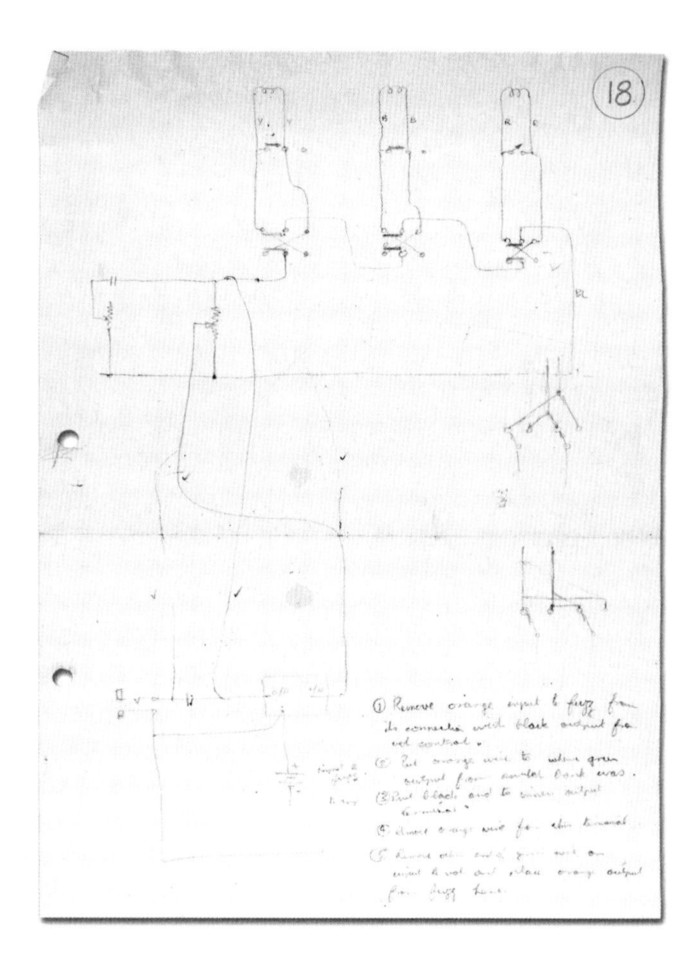

that makes the next semitone up!

Now the trick is… you multiply that length by the same factor, x, again, and you get the fret distance for another semitone up, and so on. Do it again and again with the same proportion and you get all the fret positions. But what is that factor? Well, it's defined by the fact that if you perform the operation 12 times, you get the octave, which must be half the length of the whole string. So multiplying anything by 'x' gives you a half. This is a simple equation to be solved which, in words, looks like this:

x raised to the 12th power equals a half.

Solution: x is the 12th root of a half.

A simple equation, with a simple solution, but to actually find out what the 12th root of a half actually is? Not so easy. Initially I worked it out with a slide rule, and made a table of results so I'd get the frets exactly right.

Strangely enough, when I was working at EMI Weapons Department(!) during my school holidays, I had access to one of the first computers in the world. It was the size of a small factory, but of course had much less computing power than your average smartphone of today. I wrote an iterative programme to determine the 12th root of a half, to 100 decimal places. So, if anyone wants accurate fret positions to 100 decimal places, I have them!

My philosophy in building my own guitar was different from

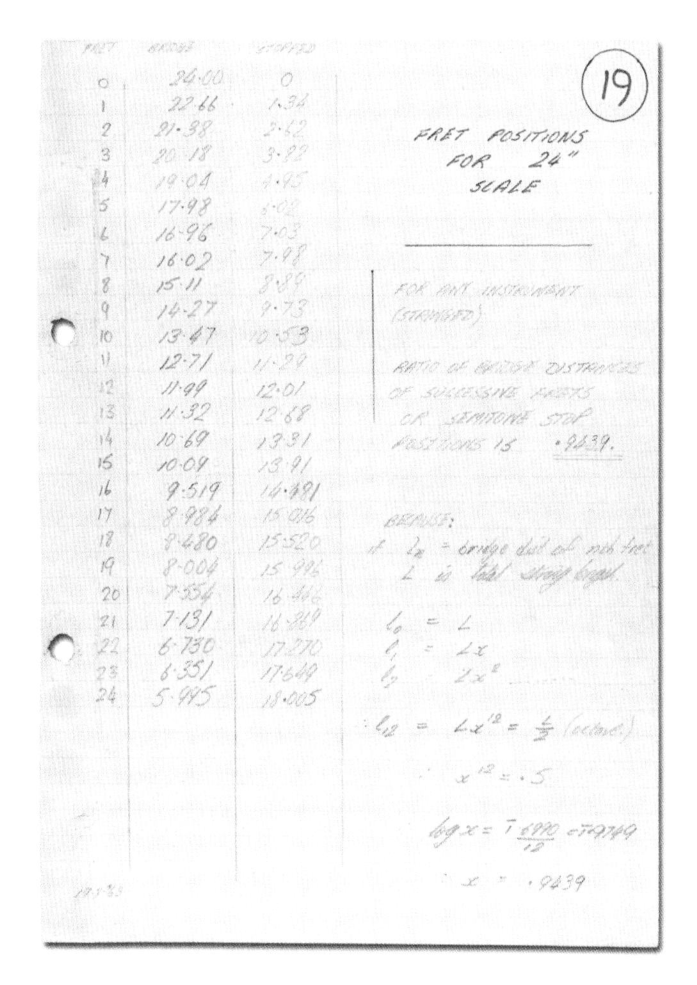

19

FRET	BRIDGE	STOPPED
0	24·00	0
1	22·66	1·34
2	21·38	2·62
3	20·18	3·82
4	19·04	4·96
5	17·98	6·02
6	16·96	7·03
7	16·02	7·98
8	15·11	8·89
9	14·27	9·73
10	13·47	10·53
11	12·71	11·29
12	11·99	12·01
13	11·32	12·68
14	10·69	13·31
15	10·09	13·91
16	9·519	14·481
17	8·984	15·016
18	8·480	15·520
19	8·004	15·996
20	7·554	16·446
21	7·131	16·869
22	6·730	17·270
23	6·351	17·649
24	5·995	18·005

FRET POSITIONS FOR 24" SCALE

FOR ANY INSTRUMENT (STRINGED)

RATIO OF BRIDGE DISTANCES OF SUCCESSIVE FRETS OR SEMITONE STOP POSITIONS IS ·9439.

BECAUSE:
if l_n = bridge dist of nth fret, L is total string length.

$l_0 = L$

$l_1 = Lx$

$l_2 = Lx^2$

$\therefore l_{12} = Lx^{12} = \frac{L}{2}$ (octave)

$\therefore x^{12} = .5$

$\log x = \frac{\bar{1}.6990}{12} = \bar{1}.9749$

$x = \cdot 9439$

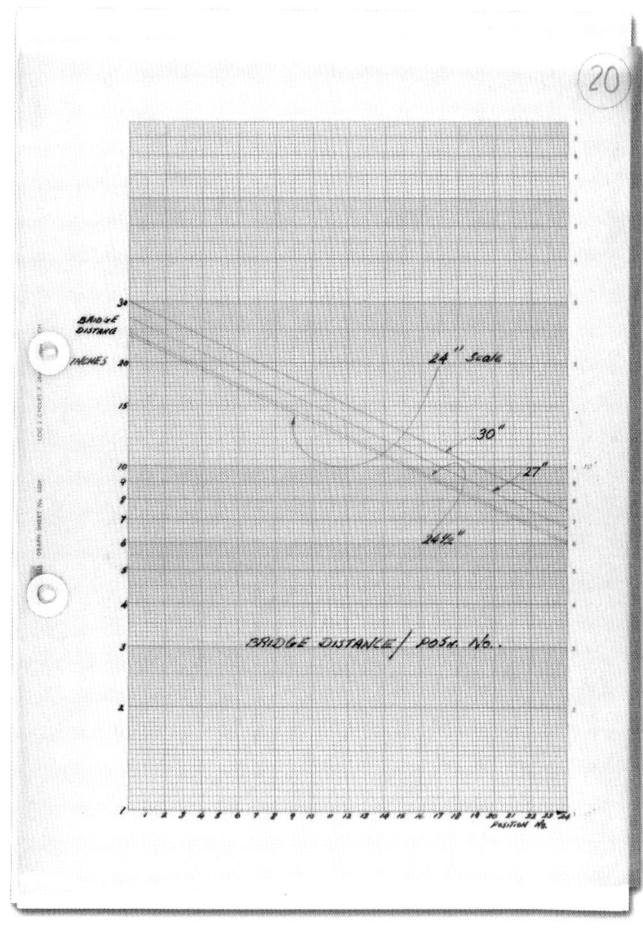

Gibson or Fender, or anyone else making solid body guitars at the time, as far as I know. Everyone had made solid body electric guitars to stop them feeding back, but in the hands of Jeff Beck and Pete Townshend, it became an instrument that was deliberately made to feedback. These brilliantly innovative guys held the guitar as close as they could to the amplifier so the vibration in the strings would sustain and actually burst into spontaneous eruption. I've mentioned the acoustic pocket in the guitar body; my guitar was designed to feedback, and I think that was a first. I wanted it to feed back in the right way, not so you'd get a booming body sound, but so it would feedback through the strings, and I hoped that the strings were so firmly anchored that it would do that. I should perhaps explain: The phenomenon commonly called 'feedback' – which can give an almost infinite sustain – happens when there is positive reinforcement in a regenerative loop. Specifically in this case, the guitar string vibrates. This sends a signal to the amplifier. The ampifier makes the loudspeaker vibrate. This vibration makes a sound wave in the air, and the sound wave – hitting the guitar string – makes it vibrate more. This makes the signal to the amp increase, and so on. It's a closed loop. To this day I don't know if it was good design or if I was just lucky, but with the Red Special, it worked. With the amplifier turned up loud, if you're in the right place, you can hit a string and it'll sustain forever, but get it wrong and the feedback will be negative – destructive – and the note will just stop. That's why guitarists like me tend to walk around the stage to find the sweet spot so the note will sustain, and to me that's the joy of a good electric guitar; it's a little difficult to control but if you get it right on a good night it becomes something magical.

I don't think the Red Special ever actually being finished! There were always little alterations going on, but it was playable before it was finished, and that was very exciting. We were able to do a lot of testing and playing around to make sure it was an instrument that was useable. I took it to school and showed my mates, and everyone was amazed, which was great! I remember taking it in even before it had strings on, imagining what it would play like one day.

Top Left: Detail of the mathematics the Mays wielded when working out the 'ratio of bridge distances of successive frets' for the Red Special.

Top Right A graph showing the distance from the bridge of each of the frets in relation to various scale lengths. The Red Special has a scale length of 24 inches (609.4mm), shorter than that of both a Gibson Les Paul and Fender Stratocaster.

Left: One of many circuit diagrams from Brian's archive that show the inner workings of the Red Special's pickups and switching system. This one mentions the Vox fuzz unit Brian fitted inside the guitar early on.

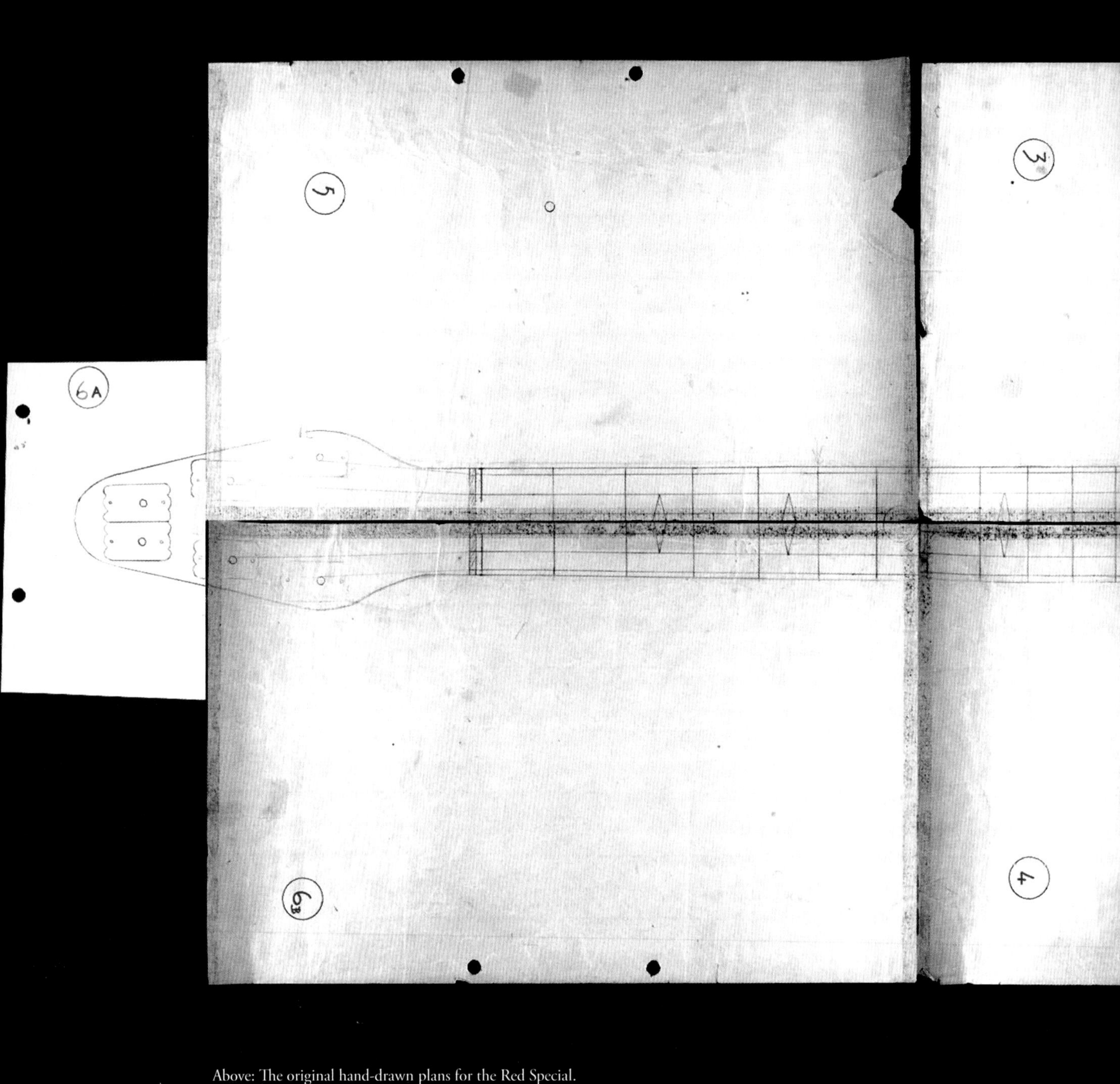

Above: The original hand-drawn plans for the Red Special. This is to scale and shows some features that didn't make it to the finished instrument, such as the f-hole and diamond fret markers. In addition, the vibrato spring cavity behind

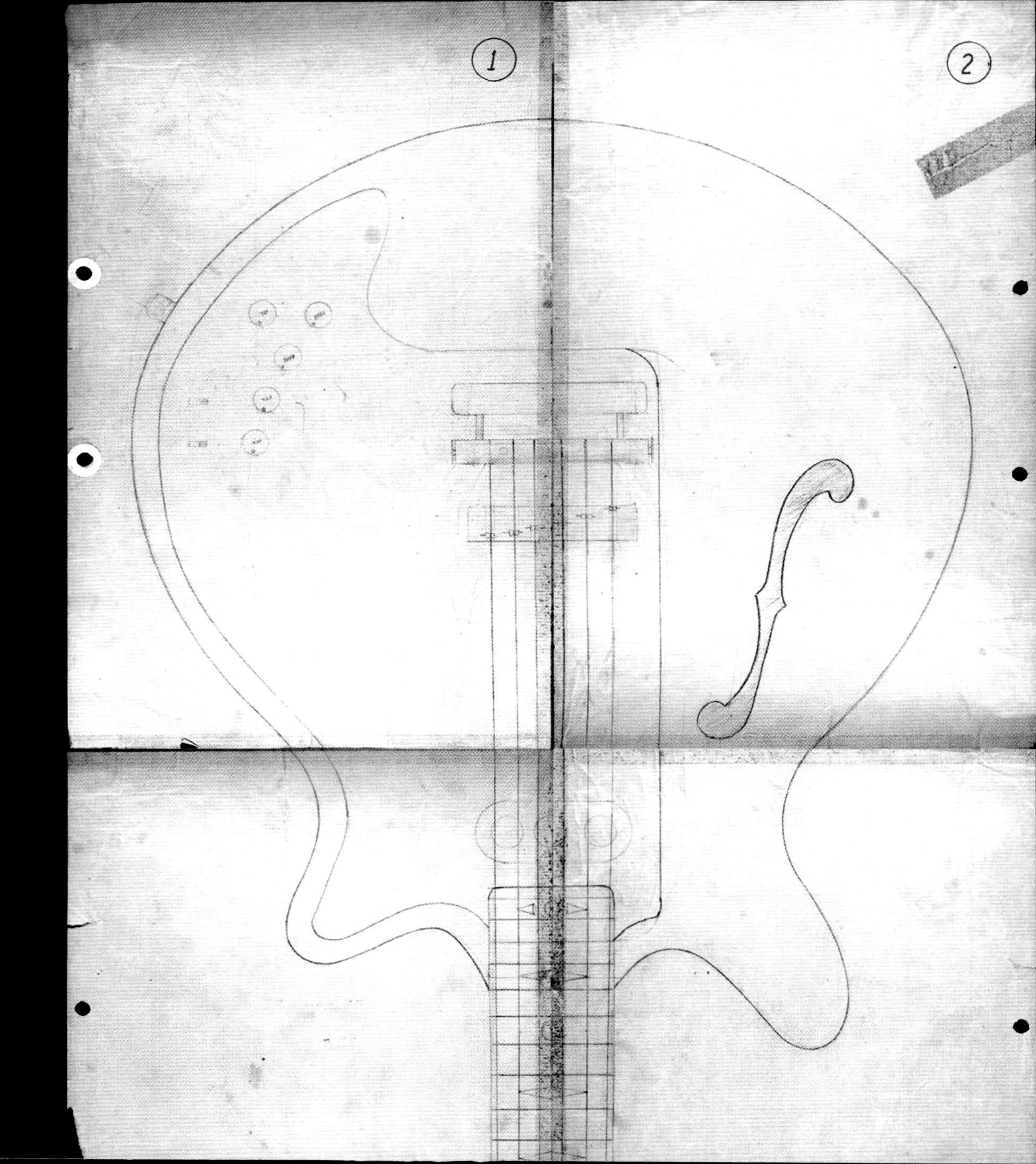
1
2

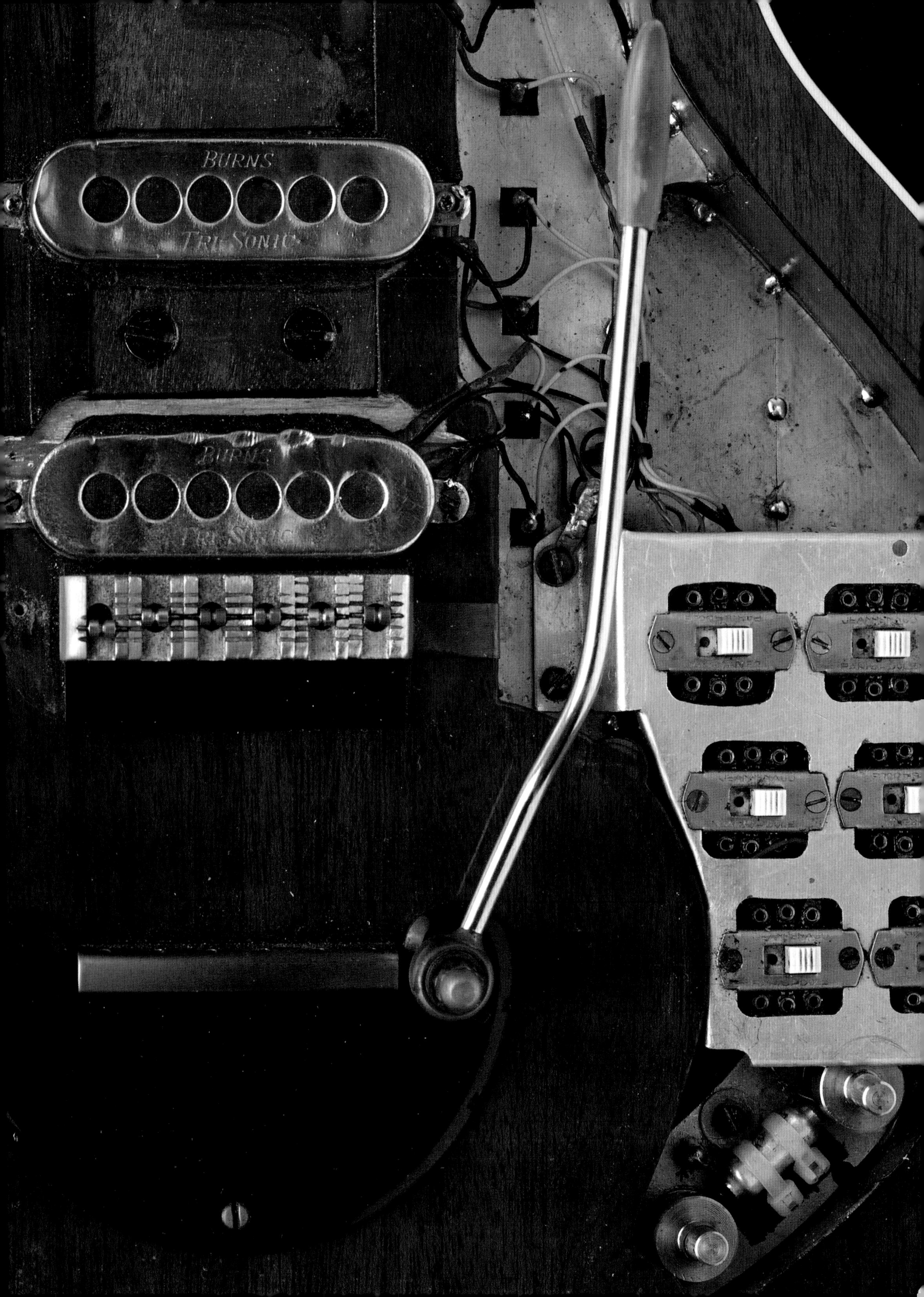
BURNS
TRI-SONIC
BURNS
TRI-SONIC

CHAPTER 3

THE WORKS: THE RED SPECIAL UP CLOSE

In this chapter Brian talks about exactly how the guitar was constructed, illustrated not only with images of the guitar in Harold May's workshop in the Sixties, but also with intimate pictures of the guitar dismantled in 2013.

THE BODY

It was going to be a semi acoustic – that was in my mind – and I thought it would have an f-hole. The guitar is largely hollow and we fabricated the body from various pieces. At the core, anchored to the neck, is an insert of very solid oak that takes the whole strain of the strings, but around it, making the shape of the body, is blockboard. Blockboard is made of various size blocks of wood all glued together in its centre, and it's surrounded with layers of plywood on each side, making a sort of sandwich. I basically chiselled out all the blocks to make the cavities of the guitar body, and left the plywood. So I went to the trouble of making it hollow, to house the electronics but also just to hold air, and that worked out incredibly well, because, as I mentioned in Chapter 2, this would be a live guitar and it would feedback. In the end I didn't need the *f*-hole that was in the original design. I could have changed my mind at any point, I suppose, as it's there on the plans, but it just seemed to work very well as it was and I thought that once I'd made the *f*-hole, I couldn't un-make it! It's an irreversible thing so it got left this way. (Andrew Guyton recently made me an arch-top version of the Red Special with an f-hole as in the original design. It also has a piezo pickup under the bridge, so it doubles as a very convincing 'acoustic'-sounding electric. I've been playing "Crazy Little Thing Called Love" on it every night on tour in the USA, as Queen + Adam Lambert, and having a lot of fun!)

I used to play with marquetry kits. They were all set up so you could make pictures out of different colouered woods. You'd get a template and lots of different veneers, and you'd cut them up, stick them on and make a picture. So I knew what veneers were and how they worked, and for my guitar, it was the only way to go. The body was this oak insert with blockboard around it and that wouldn't look very good as it was, so it needed to be faced up to make it appear like a solid block of wood. A mahogany veneer was the answer. I can't remember exactly where we would have got the veneer from, but there were various shops that used to do wood and veneers; it wasn't difficult to find.

We stuck the veneer on with Cascamite *[a powdered urea-formaldehyde resin-based wood adhesive – SB]*. It gets slightly absorbed into the wood and you have to clamp it really tightly until it's dry: that's what the bricks were all about (*See* photo on page 45). But once it's dry it'll never move again; none of that veneer has ever moved or detached itself even the slightest bit.

Above: Arguably the best known and most loved electric guitar in the world, the Red Special. Almost every single Queen song features its myriad tones in one guise or another. An exception is "Crazy Little Thing Called Love", for which Brian used Roger Taylor's late-1960s Fender Esquire.

Above: The rear of the Red Special, showing a patch of wear through the clear Rustin's topcoat caused by many years of playing and gigging. Greg Fryer refinished the entire body in 1998 as part of a major restoration process (See page 76), and signs of wear are already returning.

Right: An intimate shot of the neck pocket, showing the oak insert that takes the strain of the guitar and to which the neck is screwed. The delicate nature of the veneer is also visible, and it's staggering to think the guitar has even survived the last 50 years.

Above: July 1964. Brian and his Dad used bricks and bottles as weights to hold the veneer in place on the blockboard body while the glue – Cascamite wood adhesive – set. Once firmly secured, Brian carefully cut around the body to ensure the veneer followed its curves exactly.

Above: October 1964. The Red Special takes pride of place in the Mays' dining room on the day it was finished, surrounded by the minutiae of family life. At this point the guitar was equipped with the original control knobs, tuners and home-made pickups.

THE COLOUR

I was clear about the colour we would go for. I wanted it to be a sort of natural-ish enhanced mahogany – reddish brown – it brings out the red a little bit compared to just varnishing on to bare wood. In a sense we'd already chosen the colour by choosing mahogany for the veneer, so we used a gentle kind of wood dye and then applied lots and lots of layers of Rustin's Plastic Coating. I brushed it on and, between each successive coat, once dry, I worked with very fine sandpaper, emery paper, glass paper and finally carborundum paste until I eventually got it to a glassy finish. This was another skill my Dad tought me – the tables and book-cases he'd made all had perfect glassy finishes! The Rustin's finish sustained a lot of wear and tear over the years, and it did get some good restoration from Greg Fryer, but basically it's held up surprisingly well.

Above: That gorgeous red colour in detail. This is the rear of the guitar with the wear, inflicted preceding and following the 1998 restoration, plain to see. Brian built up layers of Rustin's Plastic Coating as a sturdy topcoat to the body's dyed-red veneer, progressively hand-sanded and polished.

Right: The grain of the mahogany veneer, still as attractive as it must have been during the build. The 'Brian May Star' inlay covers the hole in the scratchplate made to accommodate a Vox fuzz.

THE BINDING

You couldn't buy guitar body binding so what we did was find some edging that you'd put on shelves, and I cut it all down, heated it up in a bowl of warm water and gradually shaped it. I routed the body edge and stuck it on with Evo-Stik, a kind of contact adhesive. I'm surprised it's lasted so long. *[Australian luthier]* Greg Fryer did repair part of it very neatly for me a few years ago, because the guitar sustained a nasty knock, but it's basically the same as it was all those years ago. 'Purfling' we called it!

Above: September 1964. The binding around the guitar's top is still proud of the surface, indicating that Brian was yet to undertake the tricky task of cutting it back to make it flush with the Rustin's coating. The rear edge of the Red Special is also bound, and here we can just make out the hand-carved groove around the bottom edge. Binding is decorative but also practical, providing a resilient edge, and is found in many stringed instruments of differing types and styles. Needless to say, the relevant materials are widely available today, which was certainly not the case back in 1964; hence the ingenious use of shelf edging here.

Above: The binding in detail. The intricacies of such a job shouldn't be underestimated and the binding has remained largely untouched, save for some modest repair work to a small section, since 1964.

Above: Part of the bottom edge by the jack socket. Binding can offer some protection to the bodywood and here we can see that the binding, though scuffed, has saved the veneer from damage.

THE SCRATCHPLATE

The scratchplate isn't Bakelite, or PVC, but black Perspex. Perspex was better known as an early transparent plastic – a substitute for glass – but they also made it in opaque shiny black, and I just happened to find a piece. It seemed the perfect material to make a scratchplate from. It had to be quite big as I'd routed out space for the pickups and there's a big hole for the switches too. I also wanted the guitar to be easy to service, so I designed it so you can take it off and everything else is untouched, which is unusual. You undo the screws and slide it out, and all the switching and the pots stay in the guitar, mounted on a small aluminium frame. Usually you take a scratchplate off and all the bits come with it, with wires all over the place, but with this design that doesn't happen. People have sometimes asked why I didn't do it like everyone else but there is a reason; it's very useful to be able to take the scratchplate off and go in there with test meters, screwdrivers and soldering irons, and know that nothing will move when the scratchplate is replaced.

I had a Vox fuzz box that I'd bought, and I took it out of its case and put the innards inside the guitar's body. I mounted the on/off switch – a little red slider – in the scratch plate, so I had an instantly deployable fuzz tone if I wanted it. However, pretty early on in performing, I realised that what I wanted was the kind of smooth distortion and compression that you get from a valve amplifier, and the fuzz didn't do that. So after a year or so I took it out. Many years later, Greg Fryer kindly and expertly made one of my signature stars in abalone to cover up the hole.

“When I saw them play live before I went to work for them, I always thought there was a red light on the guitar. It was actually one of those sticky red dots that you'd put on a wall planner in an office, and it would always catch the stage lights: that fooled a lot of people for a long time.”

Richie Anderson, Brian's Tech 1975–78

Above: As further proof of the Mays' meticulous planning of the build, the scratchplate was specifically designed to be easily removable to allow access to the guitar's electrics and wiring. The Old Lady certainly looks rather different in this state of undress!

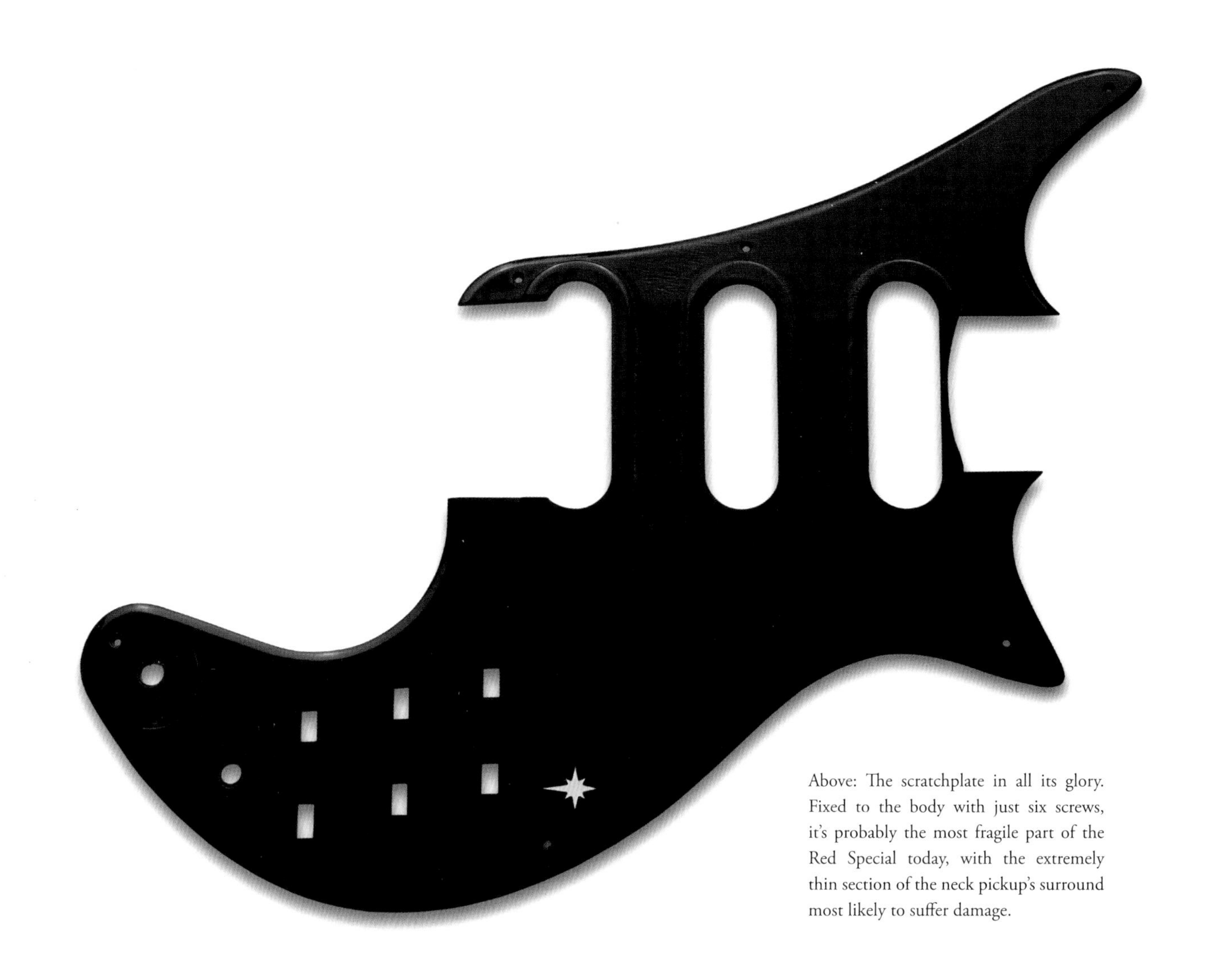

Above: The scratchplate in all its glory. Fixed to the body with just six screws, it's probably the most fragile part of the Red Special today, with the extremely thin section of the neck pickup's surround most likely to suffer damage.

Below: This angle shows the three pickup surrounds that were made by Greg Fryer in 1998 to replace the originals that had suffered serious wear. Considering the amount of use the guitar has had, the scratchplate is in surprisingly robust condition after 50 years.

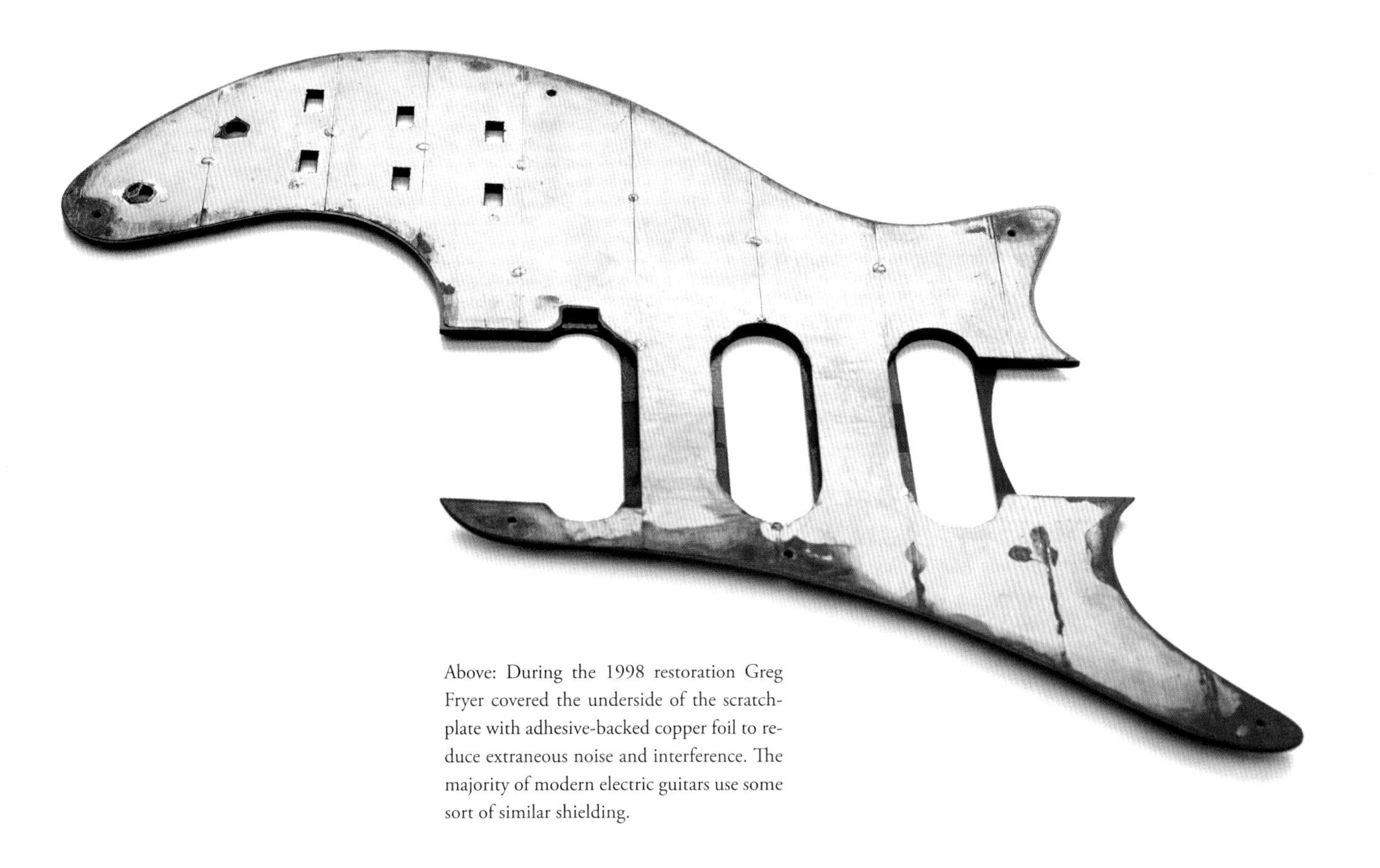

Above: During the 1998 restoration Greg Fryer covered the underside of the scratch-plate with adhesive-backed copper foil to reduce extraneous noise and interference. The majority of modern electric guitars use some sort of similar shielding.

Left: The small plate situated behind the nut that covers one end of the truss rod. Also made from black Perspex, it can be removed quickly should the neck require any slight adjustment. But the Red Special's neck is so robust it has never needed any truss rod adjustment.

THE PICKUPS

I replaced my own pickups with the Tri-Sonics as we've discussed, and they worked a treat. The Tri-Sonics have a couple of bar magnets in them, which means that the North pole is spread across the area immediately above the pickup so the string moves in a more or less a uniform field when it's 'bent' – squeezed sideways. So these pickups eliminated that problem I had had with the eclipse magnets. String bending was fine. The pickups did feedback on their own, making an unpleasant whistle, because they acted to some extent like microphones; so I took them apart and filled them up with Araldite to make them solid, and that just about fixed it. I do remember thinking about rewinding them, but found they were much improved by using the Araldite. All in all, again, whether by luck or good guidance, they became exactly what I had been looking for. They didn't quite have the crisp, sharp top end of my originals (because they had a higher inductance – more turns of wire) but the slightly warmer sound, in combination with the treble booster and AC30 worked out just great. The guitar was now absolutely useable in a concert situation – it finally had its voice.

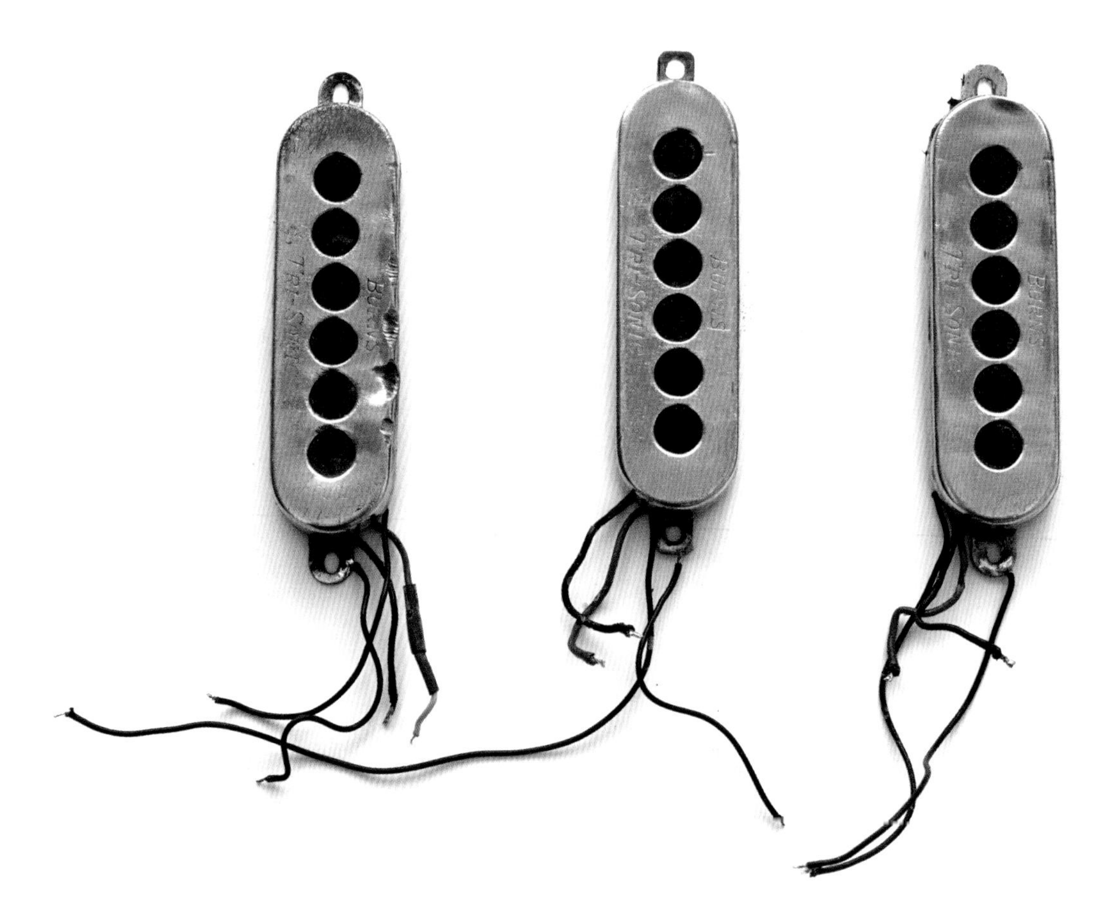

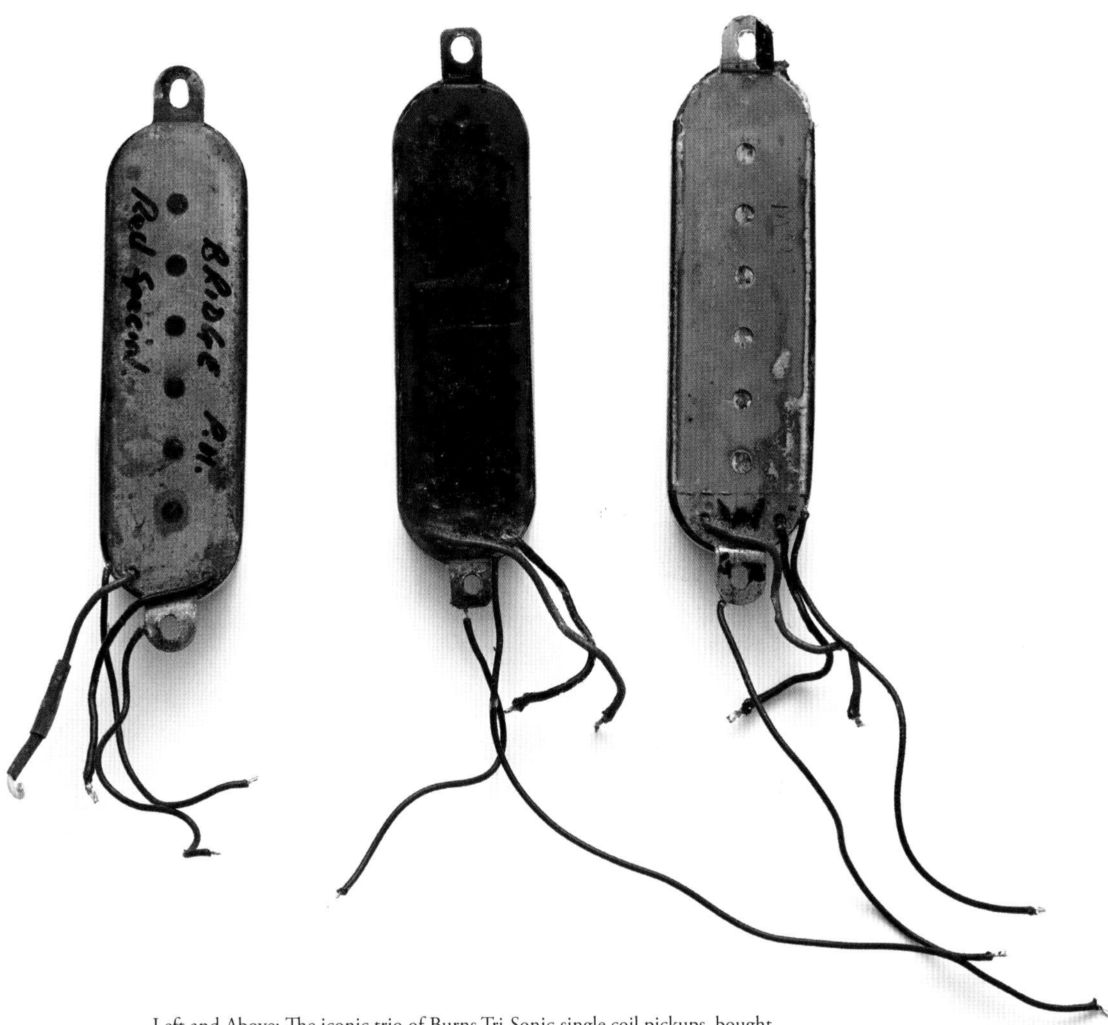

Left and Above: The iconic trio of Burns Tri-Sonic single coil pickups, bought for the princely sum of nine guineas (nine pounds nine shillings). Much has been written about these pickups and their use in Queen's various recordings and live appearances over the years, and the revolutionary switching system is addressed overleaf. The heavy wear on the casing of the bridge pickup was caused by Brian raking his serrated sixpence picks across the strings. When turned over, we can see the wires of each with more clarity and, in the case of the middle pickup, the bar magnets too.

The Red Special undergoes regular maintenance as a matter of course, but it's rare that the pickups are removed from the guitar completely, simply because of the danger of irrevocable damage occurring: it's fair to say that these Tri-Sonics are irreplaceable, irrespective of the choice of equivalents today.

THE SWITCHING SYSTEM

I had the pickups on there but the insides were all open; it was a kind of test bed – an experimental situation – for quite a long time. So I had three pickups and three sets of wires coming out, and I could wire them up in different ways. I could put them in parallel to make a particular kind of sound, by soldering all the wires from one side of the pickups together, and all the other ends together, and wire them straight up to the output jack socket. This made a very crisp but slightly hollow sound, presumably because in this configuration their collective inductance is reduced. Or I could put them all in series, which made a different kind of sound – thicker and warmer. But I also discovered an even more dramatic variation in sound was made depending on the relative phase of the pickups. I found that you could turn the polarity of any one pickup around by swapping the wires over, and if you turned one pickup around in relation to another whilst the two were in series, you got a dramatic change in sound. I was intrigued. The reason becomes clear when you realise that each pickup sits under a different part of the vibrating string, so each one picks up a different set of harmonics, depending on the

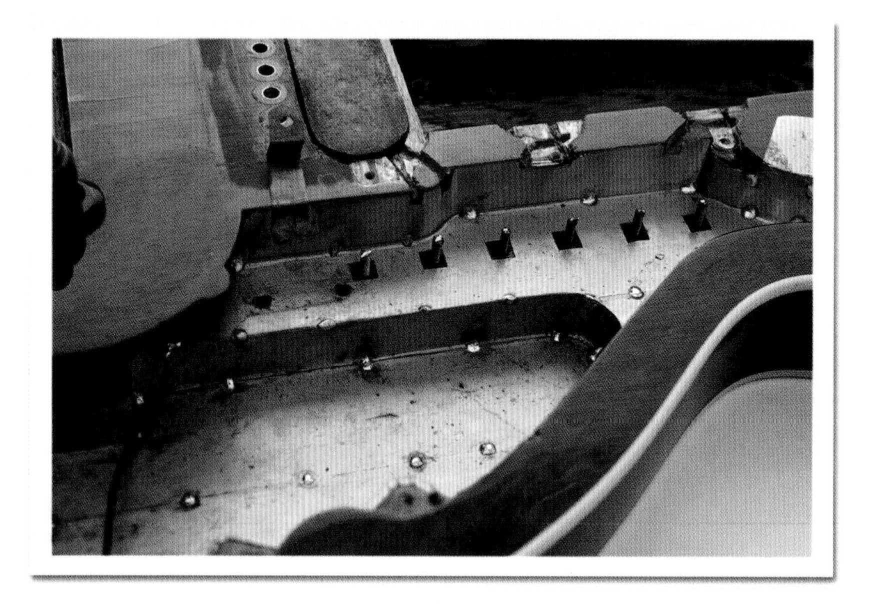

Above: The control cavity, shielded with copper foil, with the six terminals that link the pickup wires to their relevant positions within the switching system clearly visible. The pickups are wired in series, which enables them to deliver a fat tone.

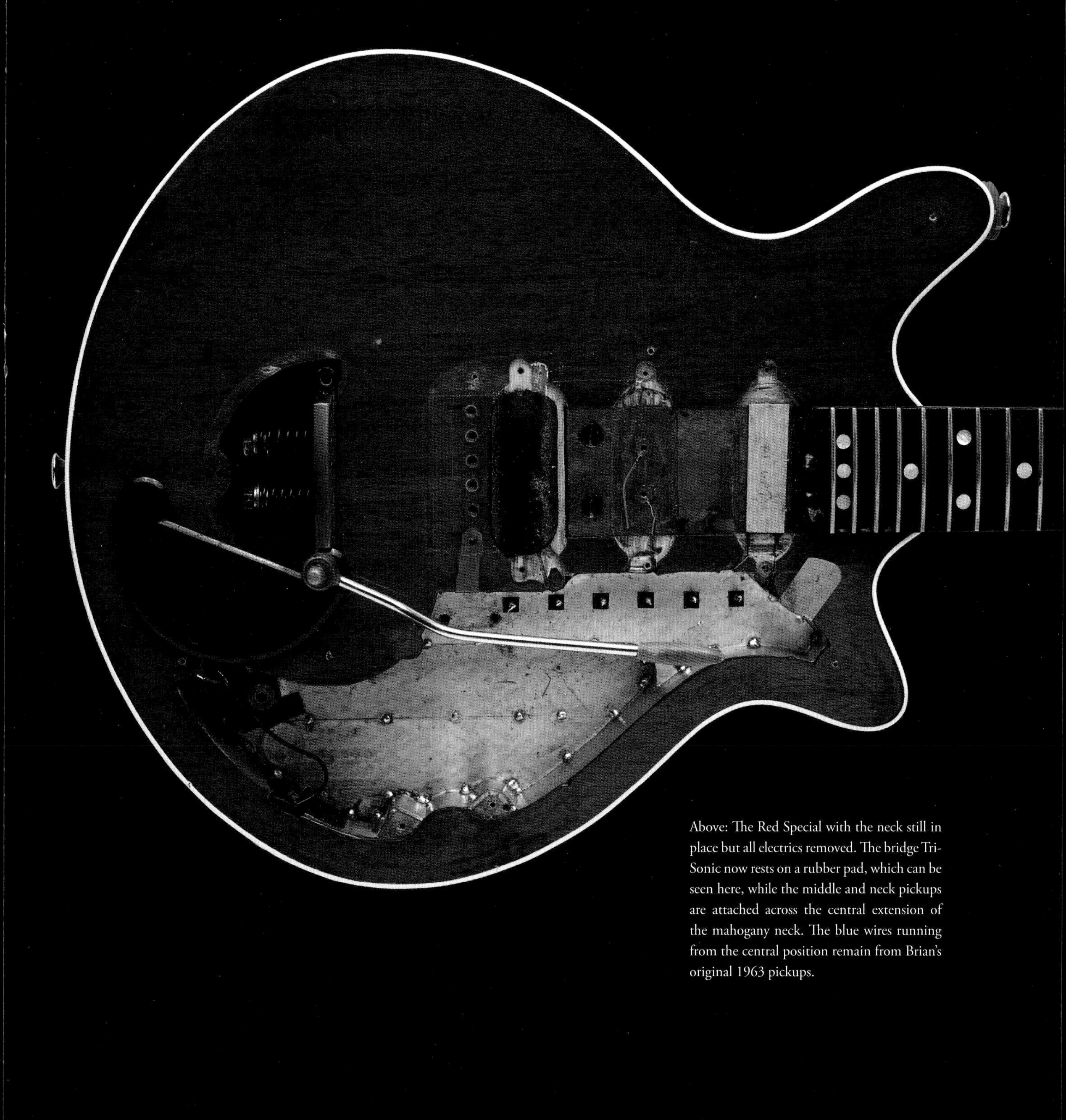

Above: The Red Special with the neck still in place but all electrics removed. The bridge Tri-Sonic now rests on a rubber pad, which can be seen here, while the middle and neck pickups are attached across the central extension of the mahogany neck. The blue wires running from the central position remain from Brian's original 1963 pickups.

amplitude (intensity) of the vibration in that frequency at that particular point on the string. Specifically, the closer to the end of the string you get, the higher the concentration of high harmonics becomes (the amplitude of the low fundamental frequency is not very much near the ends of the string – it simply can't move that far because it's anchored close by!) So a pickup placed near the bridge will give a harsh-sounding output, and one placed near the fingerboard will transmit a more mellow sound. So what happens when two pickups are wired up in phase, is that all the harmonics they pick up are added together, producing a fat, warm sound. But when they're wired *out* of phase, the frequencies they both pick up will get cancelled out. In particular, most of the fundamental note will disappear, so the resulting sound will lack the lows, and become very 'toppy' – harsh and gritty.

It's even more interesting when all three pickups are in play, and basically you go from something very warm when they're all in phase to something abrasive and full of various combinations of harmonics when they're out of phase. Every combination gives a different character... much like the vowel sounds in a human voice. To me, these sounds were precious. I didn't want to just wire it all up in one configuration and leave it, because so many fabulous sounds would be unobtainable. I wanted to harness *all* these sounds, and it couldn't be done with a regular guitar toggle switch. A new kind of switching system was needed. I decided I liked the sound of the series combinations better than the parallel ones, so I opted for parallel, and arranged the switching so that every combination of the three pickups in series could be obtained.

So in the Red Special the three pickups are wired in series, and there's a shorting switch for each of them, which takes them in and out of action – turning them on and off – and, crucially, also a phase reversal switch for each pickup. You get a lot of combinations (some redundancy too, but that's helpful when you're toggling between settings) – giving a much greater range of sounds than most other guitars. When I put the bridge and middle pickups together in phase, something special happens for me; it's hard to describe, but this setting has just enough warmth and bite to make the sound thick and solid, but there's just enough brightness to give clarity, and a healthy mixture of harmonics.

I've ended up using that sound for so many things; the riff in "Tie Your Mother Down", so much of the rhythm work I do, and a certain amount of the lead work too. But for other things, other combinations work. For the solo in "Bohemian Rhapsody", I have the fingerboard and middle pickups both on, but one is out of phase with the other, so they really fight against each other and I get these wonderful harmonics screaming out with every touch. For "Stone Cold Crazy", I use the fingerboard and bridge pickups out of phase. These two pickups are of course delivering the most widely differing sounds, so in subtraction mode, there's a lot of 'crunch' – which I love. And so on. I've used every combination in Queen's recordings, and I actually used almost *all* of them in "Bohemian Rhapsody" alone!

To my knowledge nobody had ever attempted a switching system like this, and years later I talked to one of the head designers at Fender, who was keen to try it. I believe they got as far as making a Fender guitar with this configuration but shortly afterwards, sadly, the factory burned down, and the guitar didn't survive. *[Fender's plant in Ensenada, Mexico, burned down on February 11, 1994 – SB]*

Cutting to the present day, all the guitars we now produce for BMG (Brian May Guitars) offer this whole range of sounds.

This is a digression really, but, at the best of times when you're writing a song, you hear it in your head first and it's much better to have a clear vision and try to and achieve that, rather than to just plug in and try something there and then. You need to have a vision before you start playing and, to me, that's how it's always worked best. For the "Bohemian Rhapsody" solo I could sort of hear the sound I wanted in my head and what the tune would be – I just had to get the right sound and play it. That was a sort of second lead voice and I was up against Freddie, of course. I remember him singing the "so you think you can stone me and spit in my eye" part and thinking he'd pushed himself to a new place – wow! – and the guitar had to be the same, pushing the passion to a new place; the sound, the feel and the tension in the playing. I was playing with the big boys! The Red Special never let me down – I could always find in it the voice I needed.

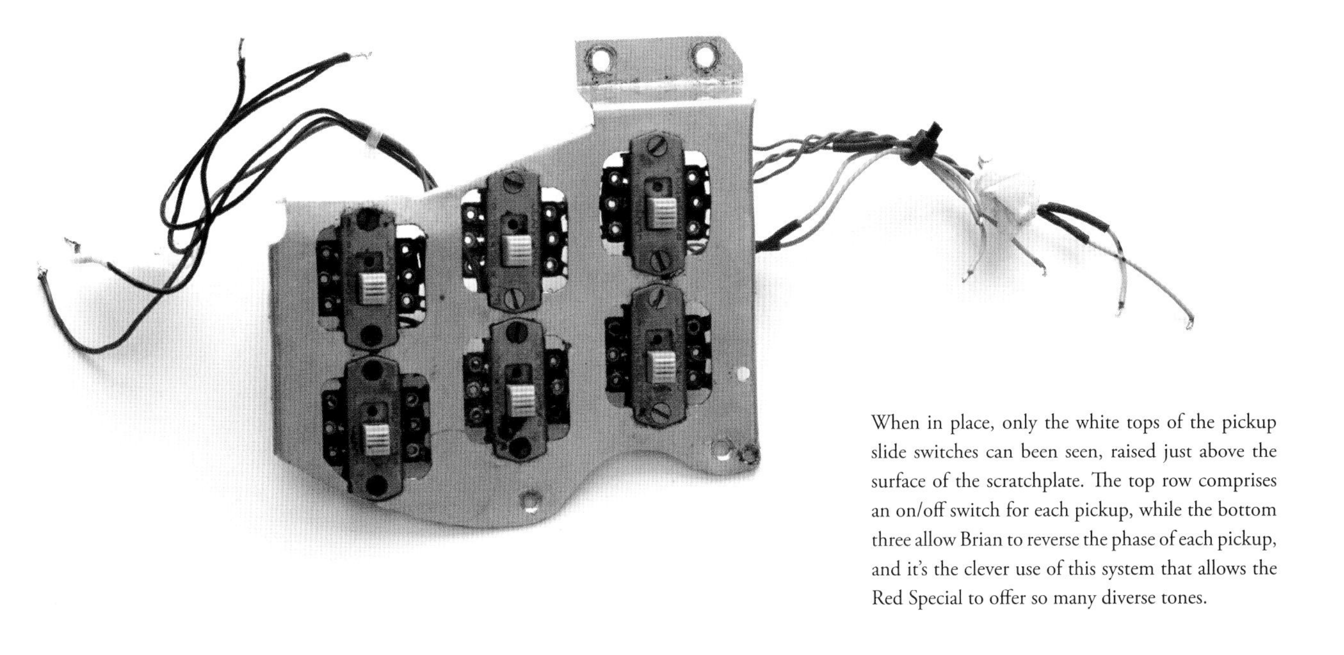

When in place, only the white tops of the pickup slide switches can been seen, raised just above the surface of the scratchplate. The top row comprises an on/off switch for each pickup, while the bottom three allow Brian to reverse the phase of each pickup, and it's the clever use of this system that allows the Red Special to offer so many diverse tones.

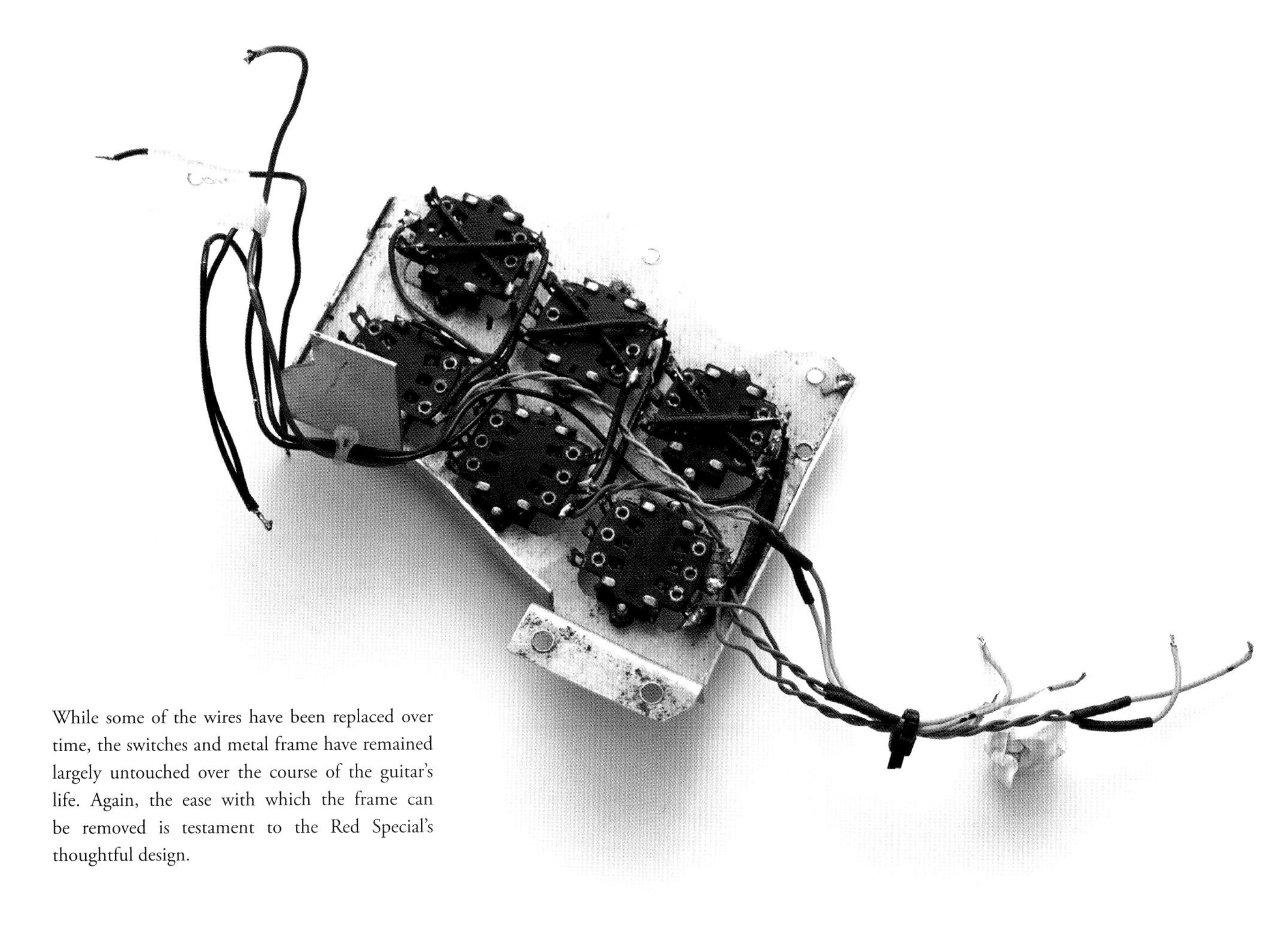

While some of the wires have been replaced over time, the switches and metal frame have remained largely untouched over the course of the guitar's life. Again, the ease with which the frame can be removed is testament to the Red Special's thoughtful design.

THE BRIDGE AND TREMOLO SYSTEM

For the tremolo system, our idea was that we'd balance the pull of the strings against the compression of two motorbike valve springs set underneath. You can tighten up the springs by putting a screwdriver into holes either side of the strap pin at the bottom end of the guitar. So if you get a perfect balance, the whole bridge assembly floats in the middle position. I have it set up so I get plenty of downward movement on the tremolo and a little bit of upward movement too. The vibrato moves smoothly and symmetrically around the zero (home) point, so it doesn't push a note out of tune. This made me happy, since in these early days I was obsessed with the way Hank Marvin of The Shadows made his guitar sound. He really was a great pioneer, and years later one of my most memorable experiences was recording with Hank. He's a monster!

I discovered that with a good tremolo you could also make aeroplane noises, whale noises, divebombs, eerie screeches, etc, which was a bonus, and that really intrigued me; I don't think anyone else was able to do that with their tremolos at that time.

I could take the bottom string down an octave and, in the days when we first went out as Queen (1970), people would be curious as to how that could happen, but it was just because the tremolo was truly floating and returned to pitch.

My Dad knew that the knife-edge, on which the bridge piece rocked, had to be case-hardened, and the rocker not hardened, so that the bearing surfaces would work themselves into a stable state; so we got a piece of steel and we case-hardened it on my mum's kitchen stove. We got this specific paste that we put on it, and it had to be heated to a certain temperature and go a certain colour, and then as it cooled, it would develop a very hard shell. So that's what we did and it hasn't been touched in fifty years. That's a well-behaved bearing!

The materials that went into the Red Special were, in so many cases, just made from things that happened to be lying around in my Dad's workshop – little pieces of steel, brass and aluminium, washers, nuts and bolts and screws, and occasionally less common objects. The tremolo arm was made from part of one of those things that support your saddlebag up on a push-bike. The tip of the arm was made from part of one of my Mum's larger knitting needles, filed down using the same method as the rollers, with my improvised lathe – a hand drill held in a vice.

Above Right: An 'exploded' view of the guitar's bridge, comprising (left to right) the soft plastic base plate upon which the array sits, two steel shims, which finely adjust the height of the bridge pieces, the six aluminium bridge blocks and six roller saddles.

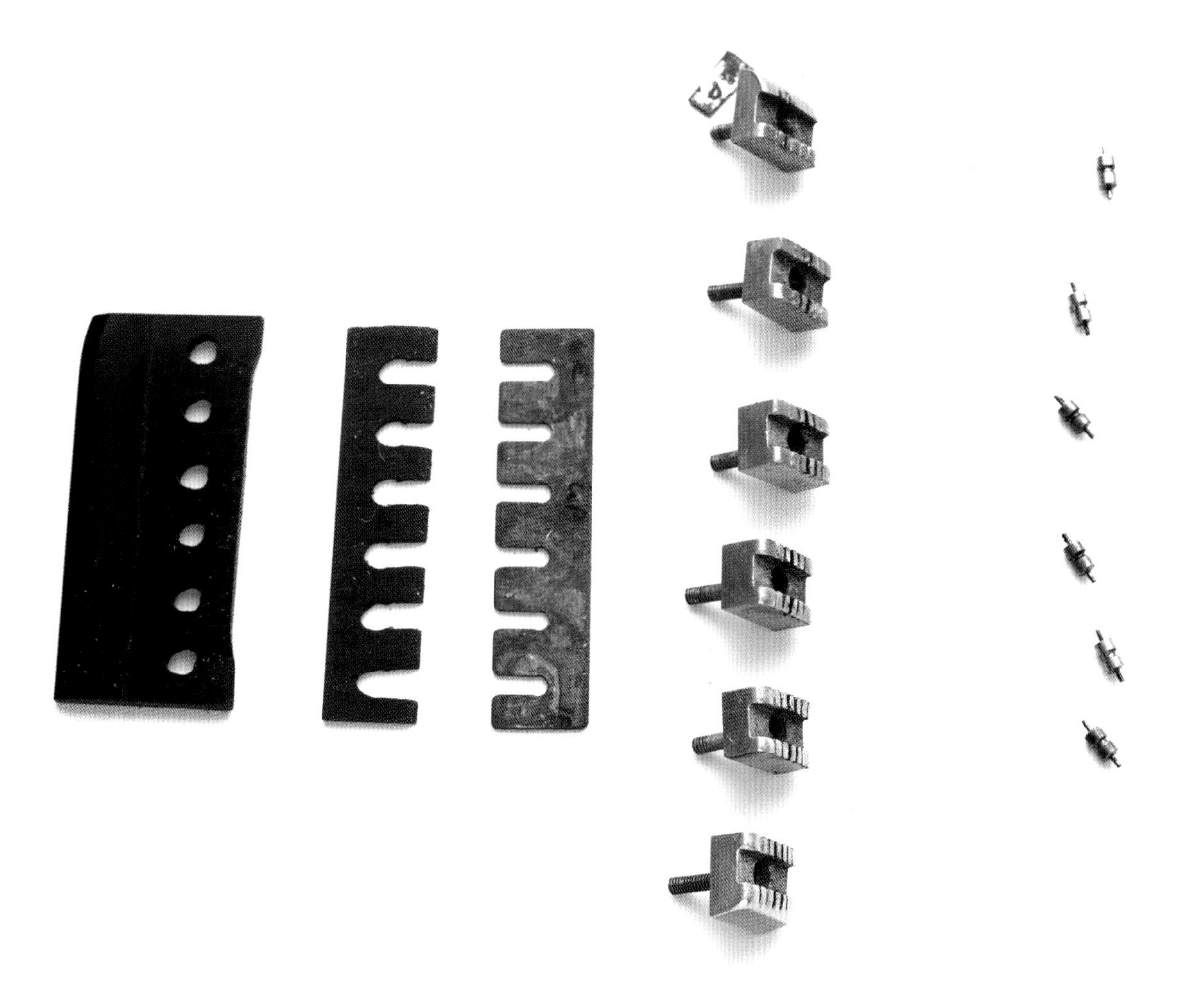

Left: Three roller saddles in close-up. Brian made the originals using a painstaking method involving a drill and hand-held file, but today he has a stock of custom-made spares that can quickly replace an errant saddle liberated by a string break.

Right: The bridge blocks of the high E and B string. Brian cut and hand-shaped all six from a single piece of aluminium and they're secured to the body by the central screw. They are all still original in 2014.

Above: The compression of the two tremolo springs can be adjusted by inserting a long screwdriver into these two holes on either side of the rear strap pin. It's an elegantly simple system that works very well indeed.

Above: The tremolo sits deep within the guitar and was the one part that we decided to leave alone, in our explorations for this book. The springs perfectly balance the pull of strings, allowing the tremolo to be truly floating.

Right: October 1963. A close-up of the two-spring tremolo design sat on a test bed in the Mays' back garden. Brian remembers that this particular design was the second arrangement he worked on. The third was the one finally adopted.

Above: October 1963. A wider shot of tremolo design Mk.2 on test, illustrating the Mays' methodical approach to all facets of the guitar's design and construction. Brian's use of the tremolo is an essential part of his playing technique.

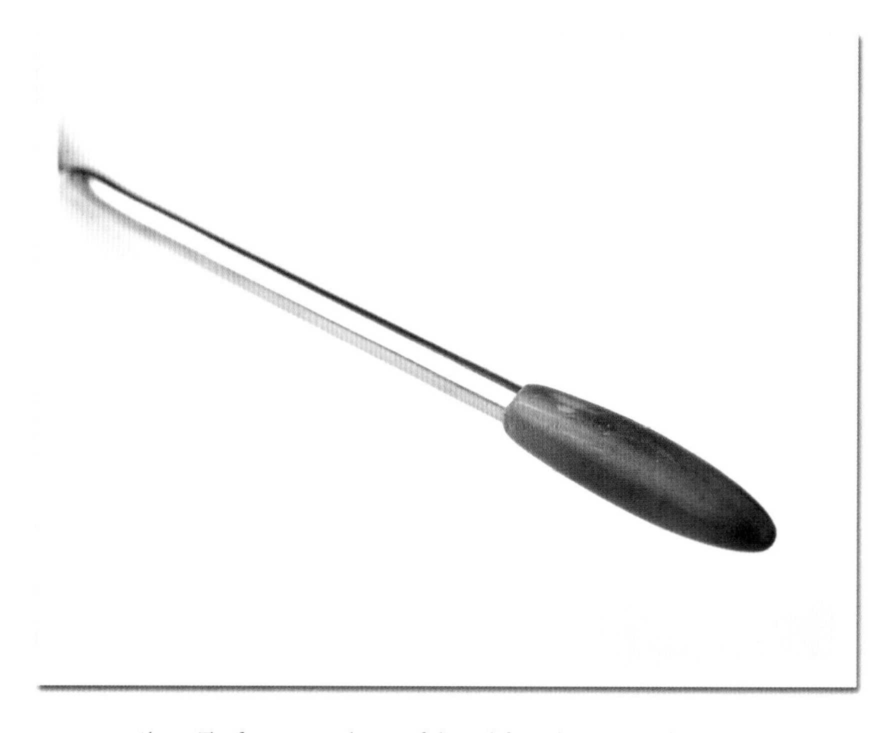

Above: The famous tremolo arm, fashioned from the support of a bicycle saddlebag and tipped with part of one of Mrs May's knitting needles shaped by Brian to just the right form, using files, emery paper, polish, and a hand drill.

THE CONTROLS

The original knobs were just cheap ones I bought in an electronics shop. Some time later at Imperial College I made some better ones, with grips and skirts with an index mark, this time on a proper lathe! They became part of the guitar just before Queen started, I suppose. The controls are just volume and tone; it wasn't too hard to figure out how to do that – for my Dad that part was child's play!

Right: Brian's self-made knobs for the volume and tone pots that have served him well throughout his entire Queen and solo career. Pictures of their predecessors show them as 1950s radio-style controls.

Left: This is the latest of a number of pairs of modern potentiometers that long ago replaced the originals, as they tend to wear out with prolonged use. They can be cleaned and maintained along with other parts, but eventually they become too noisy to be practical.

THE TRUSS ROD

There's a long stainless steel rod, the truss rod, that sits in a groove in the neck under the fingerboard and hooks around a nut and bolt that holds the neck and body together, and protrudes through the back of the body just behind the heel. I intended to put something on there to make it all neat and tidy but I never got around to it. I didn't want the neck to move at all and, my God, it doesn't move! It's like a tree trunk anyway but, with this piece of $^{3}/_{16}$ inch steel rod in it, it's never moved. It's anchored by a plate behind the nut and you can easily get in there to adjust the tension of the rod, but I've never needed to.

Above: One end of the truss rod appears just behind the nut, while the other, as shown here, extends from the neck and is secured around a bolt that runs through the body (*See* right) and out the other side, where a nut and washer keep it fastened tight.

Right: Many intimate details of the Red Special's design can be seen here: the grain of the oak insert; one of the neck pickup's terminals; the thin mahogany veneer contrasting with the more rough-and-ready nature of the blockboard; and some crazing of the clear topcoat.

THE NECK

The neck is mahogany and, if you look really closely, you can still see those wormholes that I filled up with smoothed-off matchsticks. We started by marking it all out on the front and sides of the rectangular piece of wood, and then cut it out with a tenon saw, I think. A spokeshave would have been the ideal thing but we didn't have one, so I used planes, knives, chisels and a lot of sandpaper! I gradually just whittled it away until it felt good. I was roughly aiming for the profile that my old acoustic guitar's neck had, as that was comfortable for me. Once I got going, however, I kept putting my fingers around it and it didn't actually end up quite the same. I used a bit of wood dye to stain it (along with the matchstick repairs!), and then lots of layers of Rustin's coating.

This part is funny: basically I miscalculated, because I'd overlooked the fact that the fingerboard would add thickness to the neck: it sounds ridiculous, but sometimes the most obvious things escape you. So the neck ended up thicker than I had intended, but it just felt really good. I would have corrected the oversight, because it was all together long before any finishing was done: I remember we had strings on it at one point before we started the finishing process, just to make sure that everything worked.

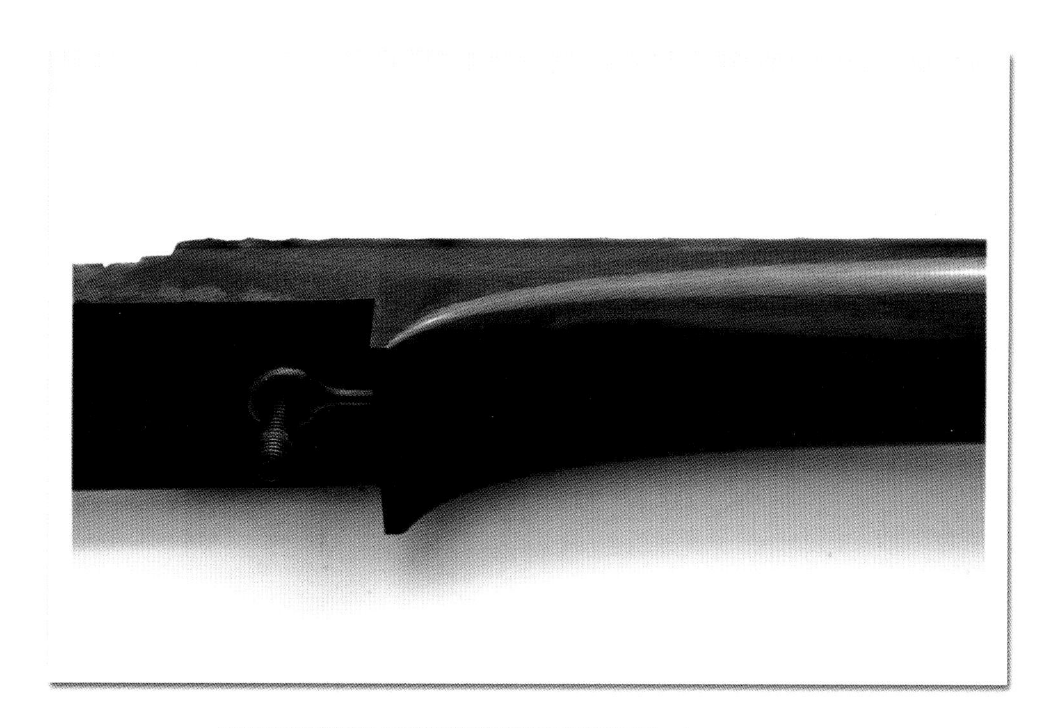

Above: A nicely angled shot that shows the shaping of the heel along with the truss rod and its securing screw. The somewhat unassuming piece of mahogany below, with "Brian's guitar neck" handwritten upon it, (Below) is the part of the fabled fireplace that remained after the neck had been made and has been in the family's possession ever since the build ended in October 1964.

Most guitarists, should they get the chance, would probably describe the Red Special's neck as "huge" and, while its width at the nut and the string spacing is fairly standard, it is genuinely massive. That said, this doesn't impact on the playing comfort and, with a mirror-smooth finish, low string action and Brian's choice of a light gauge of strings, it plays, as they say, "like butter".

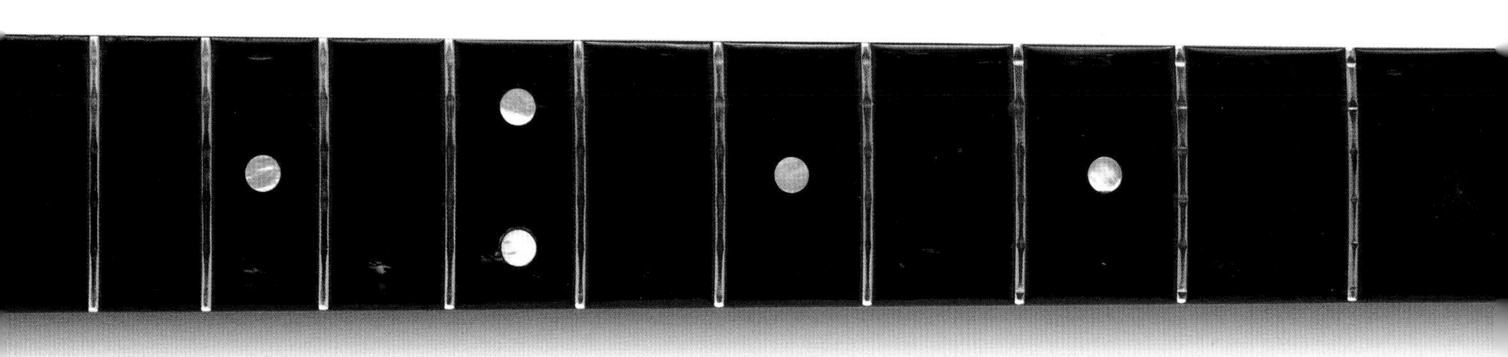

THE FINGERBOARD

The fingerboard is a separate item, of course. I carved it out from a nice flat piece of very old oak, that was extraordinarily hard, and I shaped it into a curved profile using stacks of sandpaper, to give it that gentle roundness across its width – the camber. My Egmond didn't have a cambered fingerboard – it was completely flat, but I had fallen in love with the nice easy feel of the guitars my mates had – Jag's Hofner Colorama, Wooly Hammerton's V3 – which had this very nice feature – evidently copied from the Fenders and Gibsons of the day. I don't know who first had that idea – you never find a camber on classical guitars – but thinking about it, every violin has the same feature. I really wanted ebony for the fingerboard, but we couldn't afford it, and there wasn't any kicking around the workshop, so I decided to make it feel and, hopefully, look like ebony by putting numerous layers of black plastic coating on it, the same sort of Rustin's coating we had used on the body. I can't actually remember if it came in black or if we dyed it, but I kept painting the layers on and filing and sandpapering them down until they were smooth. It had a sort of grained finish because of the sandpaper but, with use, it started to wear smooth and it's like glass now.

The combination of neck profile, smooth surface and camber make the guitar very comfortable to play – it fits my hand perfectly. I wanted my cambered fingerboard to have exactly the same curvature all the way down, so I made a template out of galvanised steel that had the correct curve. When I was planing and sandpapering down I was constantly testing it to make sure it was the right curvature at every point. If you could see daylight between the template and the wood, you'd know that there was a hotspot or a lowspot.

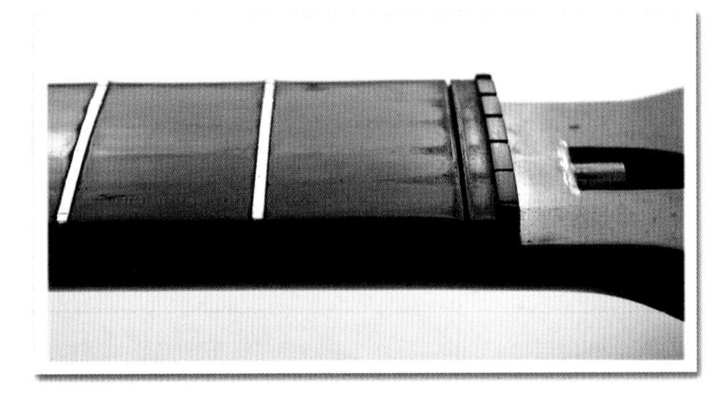

Above Left: Up close and personal with the oak fingerboard, laboriously coated and sanded to achieve its glass-like finish. Here the zero fret has been removed to show the depth of the slot.

Above Right: All frets remain perfectly seated and the Red Special has never been refretted despite some fairly hefty indents in the majority of the guitar's 24 frets, as can be seen here.

Right: The original galvanised steel template that Brian made to ensure the fingerboard possessed the exact camber – or curve – he wanted.

TO COIN A PHRASE

Brian has famously eschewed traditional guitar picks in favour of the British sixpence, again using a common or garden household object to devastating effect

Introduced in 1551, the sixpence remained in the pockets of English citizens in various forms for 420 years until its removal from circulation on Decimal Day, February 15, 1971. However, it continued to be legal tender, valued at 2½ new pence, until 1980, but by then Brian had been using the coin as a guitar pick for many years. As with the manufacture of the Red Special, he simply used what was close to hand, recalling that his mother, Ruth, used to keep a stash of sixpences in a jar in order to pay utility bills. But why a sixpence?

"The English sixpence is made of a soft metal, but it has a serrated edge." Brian told *Guitar World* in 1992. "If you turn it parallel to the strings, all that disappears because [the coin] is nice and rounded but, as soon as you angle it, the serrations give you a very pronounced attack, a splutter, which I love. It also really connects me to the string. I don't like picks that bend, because I find I'm not really in contact; I'm not really experiencing everything that happens between the pick and the string. I like the firmness of the sixpence."

The intro riff to 'It's Late' (*News Of The World*, 1977) is a clear example of the effect the sixpence has, where Brian strokes it gently across the strings to give a strangely eerie and metallic colour to his tone. In contrast, the main riff to 'Keep Yourself Alive' (*Queen*, 1973) shows how he uses the coin's serrated edge to give a starkly percussive attack, aided, in this case, by some classic tape phasing, a favourite early studio trick of Brian's.

These days genuine vintage sixpences are easy to come by, not least on eBay, where you can pick up small collections of coins for very little.

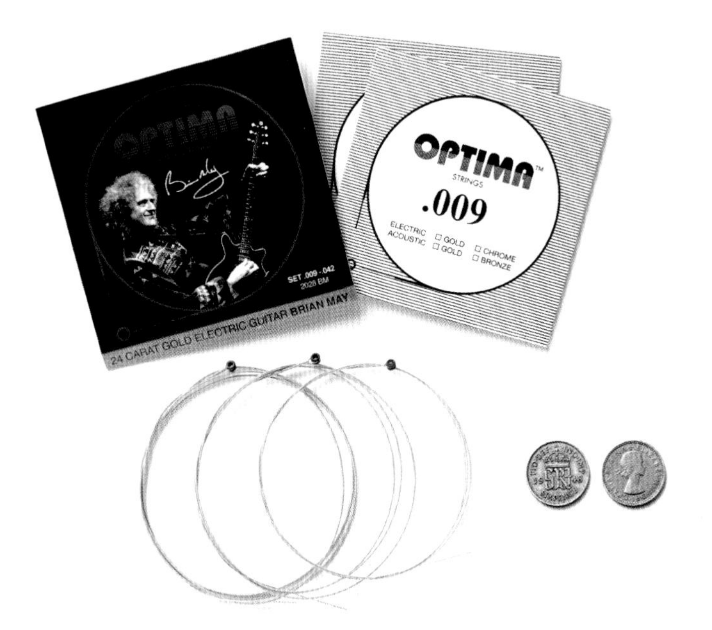

Top: The sixpence has been an integral part of both Brian's technique and tone from the very beginning, and he manipulates it to add colour and dynamics to everything he plays. Also pictured is a set of his signature Optima Gold strings (*See* page 75).

Middle: Brian favours a low action and the stability of the Red Special's neck makes it straightforward to restring. Just keep an eye on those flying roller saddles!

Right: Brian's almost unconscious technique of digging the sixpence in to the string when an aggressive feel is required has led to this unusual damage on the leading edge of the bridge pickup casing.

THE FRETS

I was keen that I'd have 24 frets, as having two octaves was logical to me. If you can't quite get all the way up it's kind of frustrating. Again, I'd never seen a guitar that had 24 frets, but I didn't see why you couldn't. That was another reason for the cutaways – so I could get to the 24th fret quite easily.

I bought the fretwire from Clifford Essex in Earlham Street, but it was very high in profile, and I wanted this comfortable low shape, so I filed every one down individually. I made jigs and templates to do that so I could file them down to the exact height I wanted. I also made a jig to form them, as they needed to be curved with exactly the right radius to fit on to the fingerboard. It took a lot of work to pre-curve the frets and bend them exactly right, because there's no point in putting a straight fret into a curved fingerboard. I evolved a tool, kind of by trial and error, to bend the fret in a vice to just the right shape – I was quite proud of that at the time!

Then you have to glue the frets in, so I made a series of gluing blocks that had rubber on one face and nails knocked into the sides. You'd put the glued fret into the slot on the fingerboard and use rubber bands that wrapped around the nails to hold the block in place until the fret glue was dry.

Funny thing is, I mapped them all out as I've described and made all the cuts with my saws – I had a measured template for that too, with grooves at each end so the saw would be in exactly the right place – and then I found I'd made a mistake: one was a 1/10 of an inch out, which is a lot. So I had to fill it in and redo it.

The Red Special has never been refretted either, which astounds people. The only thing I've replaced is the zero fret with a spare that I had in a box: everything else is original and it's a miracle that it's all still OK.

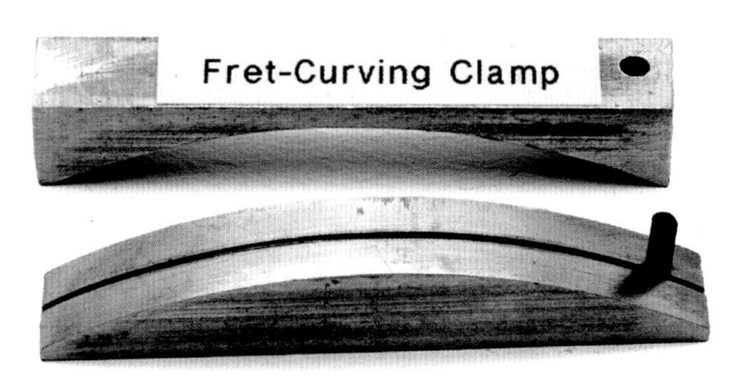

Left: The potentially tricky process of gluing each fret in place was made far simpler by Brian's ability to design and build just the right tools for the job. Here, in the May's back garden, frets 21 and 22 are secured.

Above: The home-made tool that allowed Brian to apply just the right curve to the Red Special's fretwire. Brian was particularly proud of this invention.

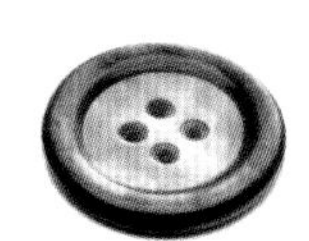

THE DOT MARKERS

The dots were made from buttons for shirts that my Mum had saved in a special mysterious button box, which had been very much part of my childhood. They're beautiful things and real mother-of-pearl is never the same twice. I saved the most colourful ones to go on the 24th fret and they're almost like the aurora colours: there's an aurora green, a sort of purple-red too. They were all fitted by hand and I had to cut the holes out by hand as well. They were my Mum's buttons and she was very good about it, very happy to help! I still have some of those buttons somewhere.

Above: Not even Ruth May's sewing box was safe, with her supply of mother-of-pearl shirt buttons plundered for the fingerboard's dot markers. Of all 16 that stud the Red Special's fingerboard, the green button at the centre of the 24th fret's trio is the most striking. "The 12th and 24th fret are marked with three dots, to make them distinctive and easy to see – which, as far as I know, was never done before," explains Brian.

Above Right and Left: Some of Mrs May's original pearl buttons. Their sewing box counterparts were, of course, meticulously shaped by Brian and used as the fingerboard's dot markers.

THE NUT

We spoke about friction being an obstacle to the strings returning to pitch after tremolo movements. The roller bridge took care of this problem at the bridge end, but the last area to eliminate friction was at the other end, the nut, where the strings are located near the machine head (tuner) area. They make roller nuts these days, but I solved the problem in a different way. In those days strings generally went through the nut at a sharp angle because they needed to be anchored, but I thought the way to do it would be to have them go through at a very shallow gradient so there wouldn't be very much friction anywhere. Basically there's no bottom to the slots in the nut; the strings just float in the nut, located vertically by the zero fret. I positioned the machine heads on the head of the guitar so that there was almost no lateral deviation of the strings as they passed through. This was only possible because I didn't use the one-sided kind of headstock that Fender employed, but made the head shape a kind of tapering lozenge shape – exactly for this pupose. And it was only possible because, unlike most commercial guitars at that time, the nut was separate from the zero fret. Where did that idea come from? The old Egmond!

THE HEADSTOCK

The headstock might look like a whim, but, as we've seen, it was designed to allow the strings to go almost straight laterally as well as vertically so they don't rub on the sides of the nut's grooves. As a low-friction unit, it turned out pretty successfully: it needs a little application of graphite now and then, as most guitars do, but basically the guitar has always been quite good at returning to pitch. In the early days I used to find strings going badly out of tune, but we traced this to problems with the machine heads.

In fact those original machineheads were the only other commercially made item that I bought for the guitar in its first state, because I couldn't make them. I'm pretty sure they were from Clifford Essex as well, but they didn't last that long, so I've had many replacements over the years; most recently some chrome Schaller locking M6s with pearloid buttons. They're nice because they lock the string, which really helps the tuning.

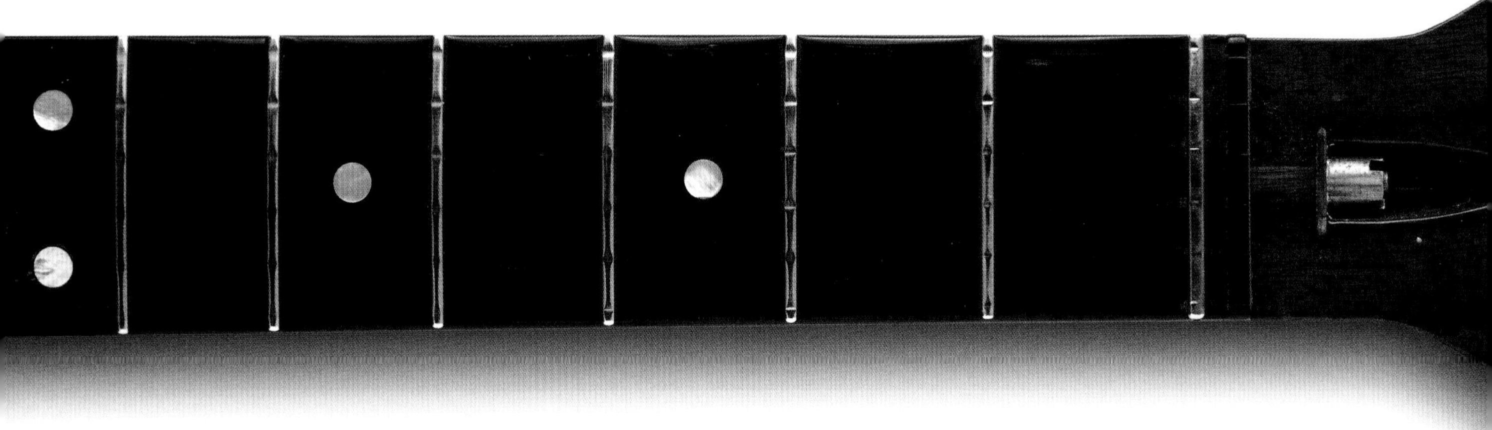

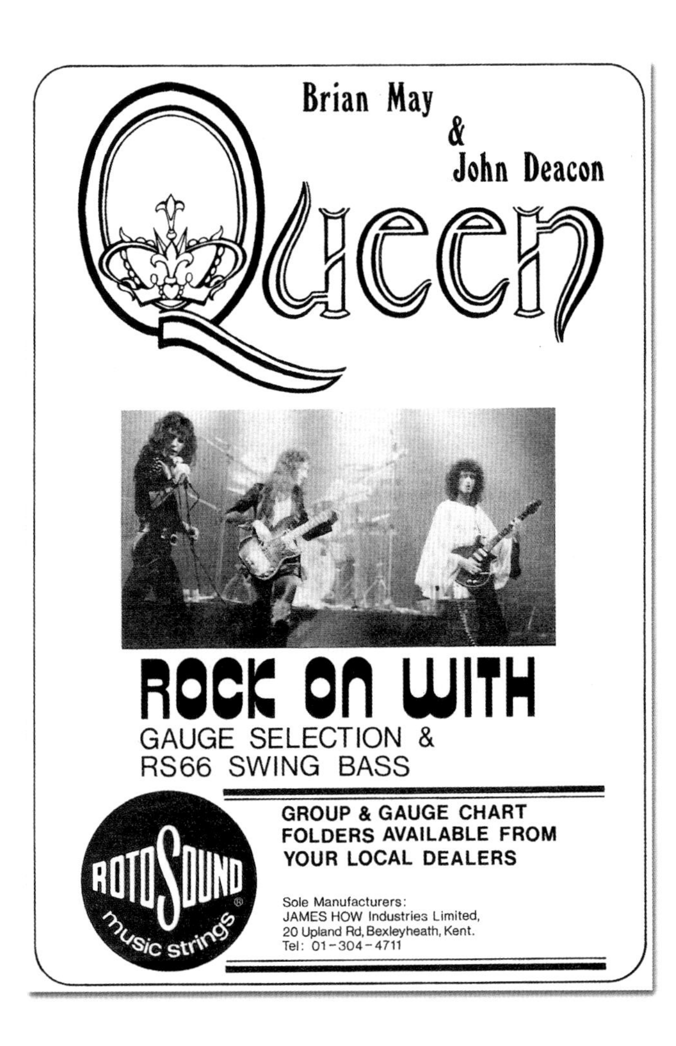

STRINGS AND THINGS

Brian's choice of guitar string – with Pete Malandrone

Brian has always opted for a light gauge, or thickness, of string and, during the band's rise to glory during the mid-1970s and beyond, used custom gauge selection sets of stainless steel strings from UK maker Rotosound. Queen bassist John Deacon also used Rotosound strings, specifically custom-made Superwound sets, and Queen crew member Pete 'Ratty' Hince remembers that the gauges of strings used on the Red Special in those days ran .008, .010, .011, .022, 0.30, and .034, high to low.

What's more, Brian famously doesn't like the tone that brand new strings unavoidably give, as guitar tech Pete Malandrone explains: "He doesn't really like the sound of new strings, so I would never change all six at once in normal circumstances as it does make the guitar sound very different." *[Brian's reaction to this: "I love the sound of new strings – I just don't trust them to stay in tune!"]*

"Brian doesn't break as many as you think he should, playing with a coin," he continues. "On tour he'll maybe break something like one every three shows, but it's never the same one."

Today Brian uses his own signature packs from Optima, the Optima Gold 2028BM set, which comprises strings with a steel core plated with 24 carat gold. They have a slightly heavier gauge too, running .009, .011, .014, .024, .032 and .042, high to low. The set was made commercially available in 2006, although Brian joined up with Maxima, as the company was known, around 1990.

Left: Even the classic three-a-side headstock design benefitted from some forethought, and it works in tandem with the tremolo to ensure that the Red Special's tuning remains stable. The locking machine heads are a recent addition, with the pearloid buttons fitting the vibe nicely, and Brian himself glued the 'May Sixpence' to the headstock. This picture also shows the state of the frets, with many demonstrating grooved dents, but such is Brian's lightness of touch as a player that he has no need to change any of them.

THE FIRST RESTORATION

“In 1998, the Red Special underwent the first full-scale restoration of its eventful life. Brian recalls how the work began before the man who took on this daunting task, Australian luthier Greg Fryer, takes up the story.”

Greg wrote me this letter from Australia,” Brian explained to *Guitarist* magazine in 1998, “and said that the pinnacle of his life would be to make a proper copy of the Old Lady. I talked to him and he flew himself over, and I let him go over the guitar to the ultimate millionth of an inch; he went home again and 18 months later arrived with three superb copies of the guitar. Greg did it all by hand exactly the way I'd done it, and if I'd gone looking for someone who could do this, it would have taken years to find him.”

Here's an overview of just some of the procedures undertaken during the restoration, courtesy of Greg Fryer.

“At times it was nerve-wracking handling such a legendary instrument. Even at the most difficult times I realised that it was a tremendous privilege to be working with Brian and that I had great responsibility to be as consistent and reliable as possible.

“I addressed a number of repairs in different areas, all with Brian's approval. At the time he was occupied by the recording of *Another World* (1998) and couldn't assist in the repair processes, so, at the beginning of each day he and I would discuss the repairs and the priorities over a cup of tea. He would usually pop in during a break in recording to see how things were going too.

“The Tri Sonics were taken apart and each had their brass covers panel-beaten to get them flat again after years of being pounded by Brian's sixpence. The coils and baseplates were then reassembled

and finally the whole pickup was soaked in a paraffin wax solution for further feedback reduction. I also made three new surrounds from 3mm black Perspex and filled the rectangular hole in the scratchplate where a switch for the original fuzz unit had been. I glued in a piece of black acrylic, sanded it flat, hand polished it and inlaid a mother-of-pearl 'May Star'.

"I replaced the fifth fret dot with a new mother-of-pearl, shaped by hand using the same tools and method that Brian had originally used, and cleaned up and polished the tremolo tailpiece. I also fitted new bridge rollers and made a number of spares.

"The body binding was barely hanging on but, considering that the guitar had been used solidly for over 30 years by that time and all around the world, it was in surprisingly good overall shape especially given the extremes of temperature and humidity that it would have encountered. Harold and Brian had made a very solid and dependable instrument."

Opposite: All the work was conducted at Brian's Allerton Hill studio near London, and many of the tasks were either assisted or supervised by Brian. Here he closely examines one of the new dot makers under a microscope.

Above: Greg's workbench at Allerton. "Some of the repairs were scary and difficult, and most required materials and techniques that I had not previously encountered in conventional guitar repair." he says. "It was certainly very helpful having Brian around."

Left: The Tri-Sonics undergo a process called 'wax potting', where the pickups, complete with cover, are soaked for 45 minutes in a paraffin wax solution. This significantly reduces feedback by holding the coil perfectly rigid and removing all air from within.

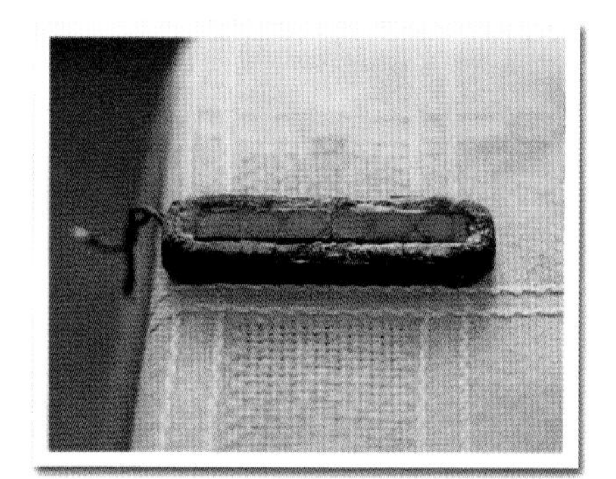

Above: The three pickups in a severe state of undress. "They were giving Brian difficulty at high volume levels and causing microphonic feedback. Vibration in and around the pickup and its metal cover was causing the problem, so it was my job to work out ways to improve this."

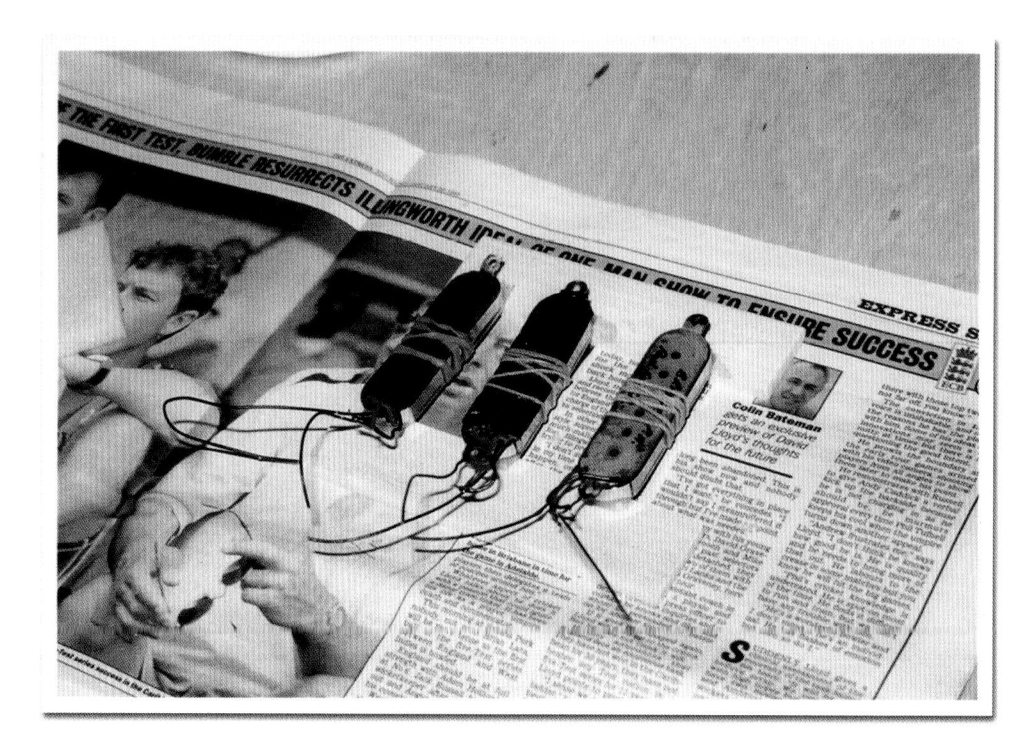

Right: After the potting process, the pickups are laid out to dry. "The brass covers were panel-beaten to get them flat and straight again after years of being pounded by Brian's sixpence. The coils and baseplate were then reassembled."

Authenticity was always at the heart of any repairs undertaken. "I replaced the fifth-fret dot with a new mother-of-pearl dot, which I shaped by hand using the same tool and method that Brian used to make the original fingerboard dots from his Mum's pearl buttons."

At end of the fingerboard by the 24th fret, chewed up by almost constant use. "The Red Special was in need of repairs to many areas, although considering that the guitar had been used solidly for over 30 years of live playing around the world, it was also in surprisingly good overall shape – especially given the extremes of temperature and humidity that it would have encountered."

Here the scratchplate gets some much-needed TLC. "A section that had broken off was reglued and, to reinforce the break, I inlayed a black acrylic (Perspex) piece and brass sheet. I then fine-sanded and hand-polished the surfaces to look the same as rest of the scratchplate."

"Some areas of the guitar, such as the white binding, needed immediate attention because it had become unglued and was barely hanging on; same with the mahogany veneer which, in several areas, I either repaired or replaced. At times it was nerve-wracking handling a legendary instrument that wasn't insured, worth millions of pounds, irreplaceable and much of it in delicate condition."

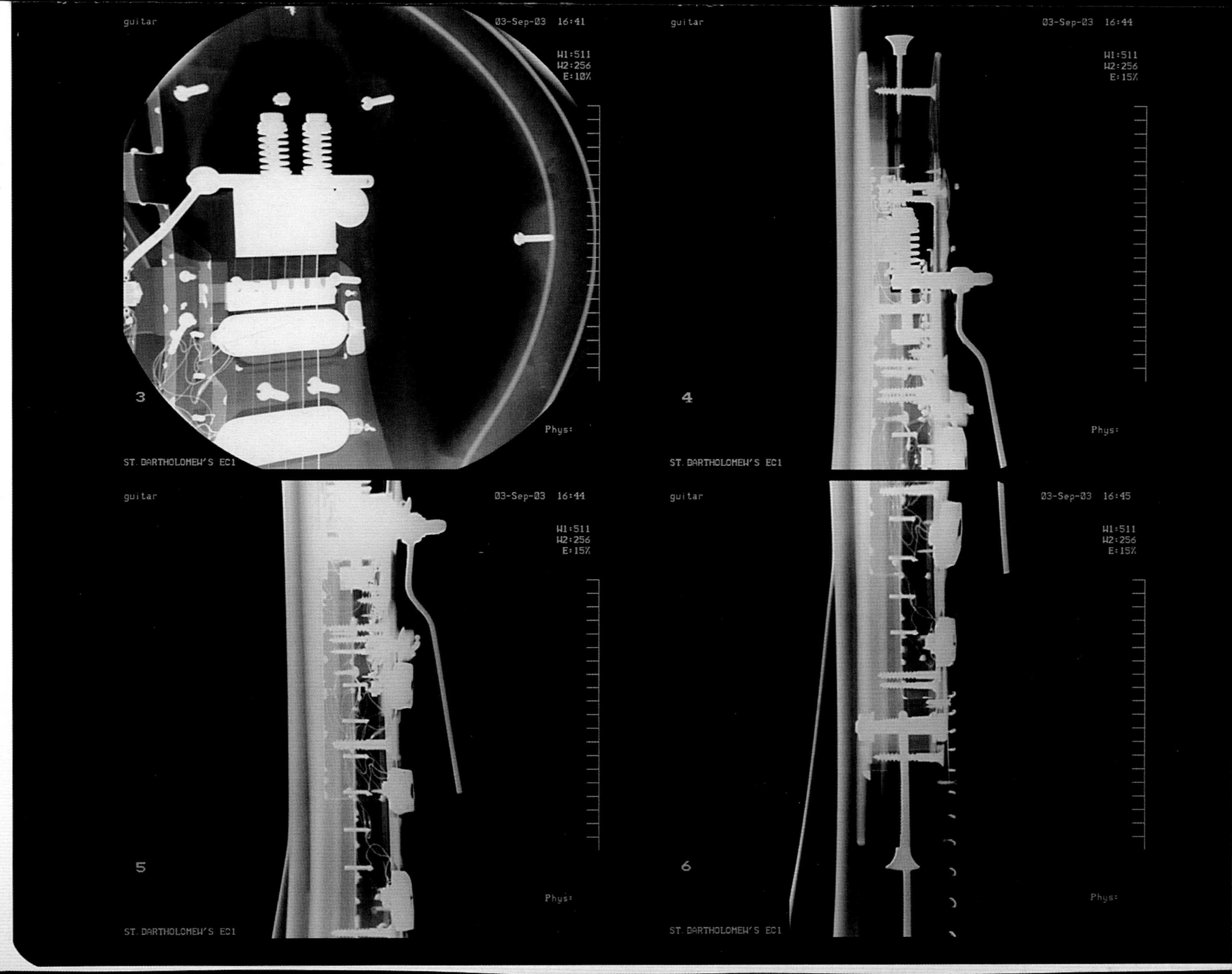
guitar
03-Sep-03 16:41
W1:511
W2:256
E:10%
3
Phys:
ST. BARTHOLOMEW'S EC1
guitar
03-Sep-03 16:44
W1:511
W2:256
E:15%
4
Phys:
ST. BARTHOLOMEW'S EC1
guitar
03-Sep-03 16:44
W1:511
W2:256
E:15%
5
Phys:
ST. BARTHOLOMEW'S EC1
guitar
03-Sep-03 16:45
W1:511
W2:256
E:15%
6
Phys:
ST. BARTHOLOMEW'S EC1

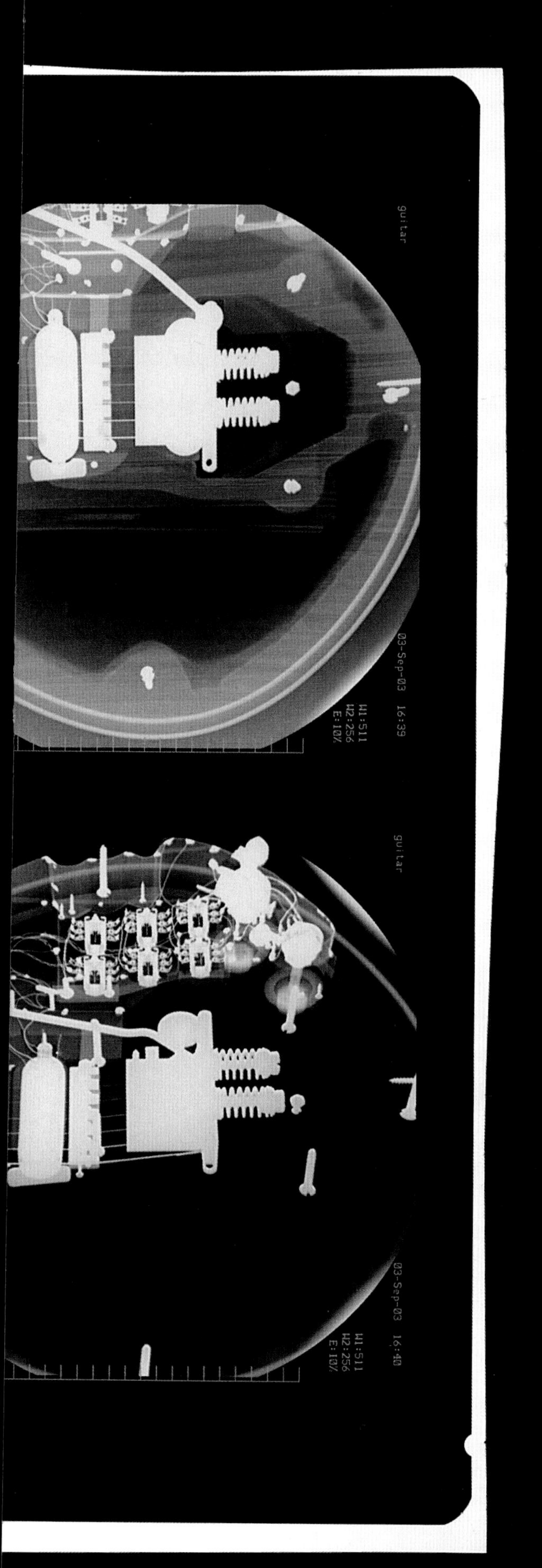

Above and Left: Some revealing x-rays of the Red Special, including several that have been unpublished until now. Amongst the fascinating detail is the series of screws that hold the two halves of the blockboard body together, the body's acoustic pockets and the truss rod – all conceived, designed and built by Harold and Brian May.

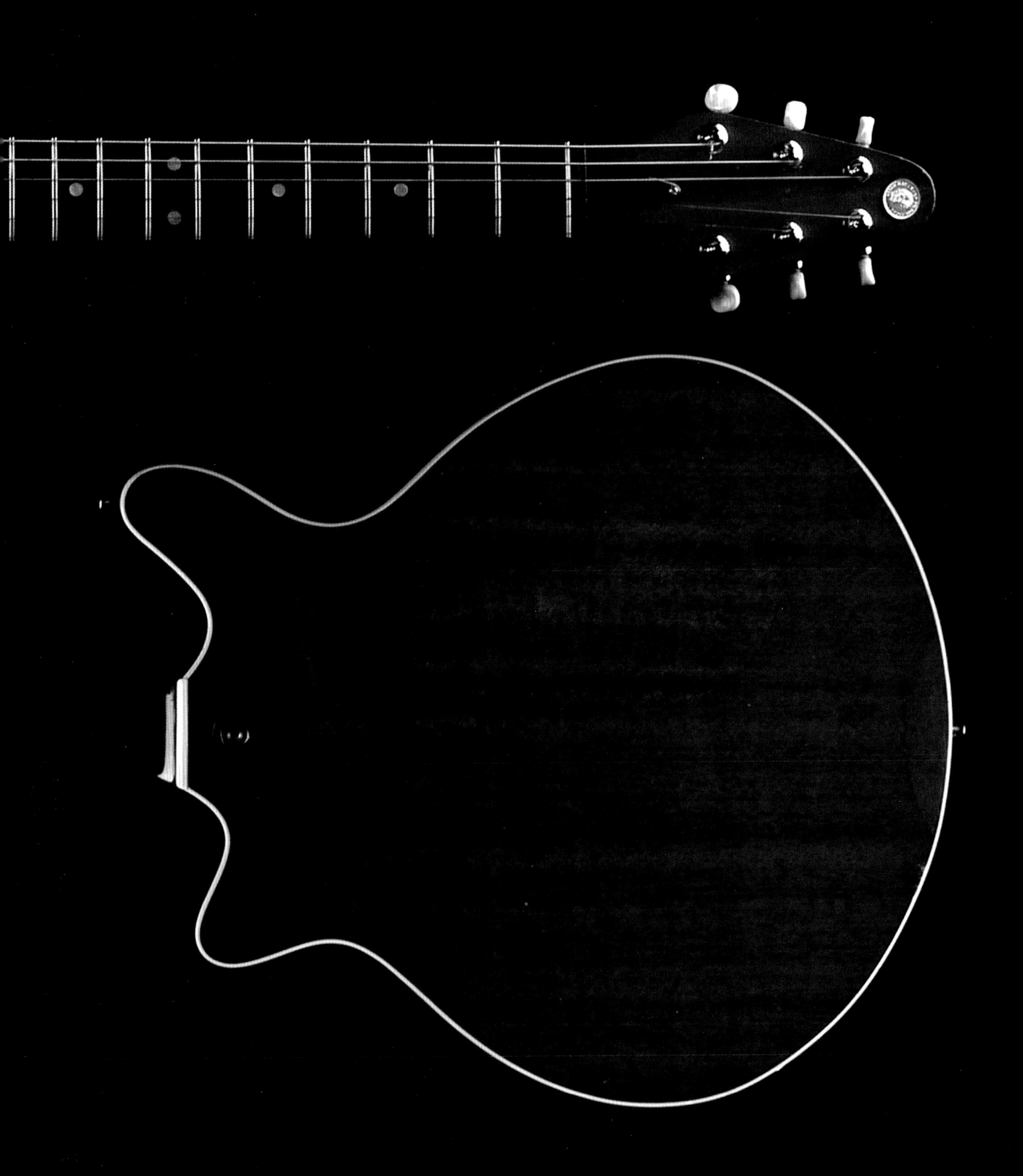

RED SPECIAL SPECIFICATIONS

An at-a-glance rundown of the Red Special's vital statistics

Body thickness: 40mm (+/- 0.5mm)

Body: Chambered blockboard with central oak insert, mahogany veneers, white front and rear binding, and black Perspex scratchplate, pickup surrounds and vibrato cover.

Neck: Mahogany

Scale length: 609.5mm (24")

Fingerboard: English oak, painted with black plastic coating, 16 pearl button dot markers, 184.15mm (7.25") radius

Width at nut: 46mm

Width at 12th fret: 50mm

Width at 24th fret: 53mm

String spacing at bridge: 51.5mm

Strings: Optima Gold 2028BM, 009 -.042 gauge set, steel core plated with 24 carat gold

Frets: 24 plus zero fret

Pickups: Three Burns Tri-Sonic single coils, wired in series

Controls: Volume and tone pots, plus three on/off pickup switches and three pickup phase reversal switches

Hardware: Aluminium bridge with individual steel roller saddles, sprung vibrato tailpiece comprising mild steel block and case-hardened steel knife-edge, aluminium control knobs, and Schaller locking M6 tuners

Weight: 3.63kg / 7.99lbs

Finish: Mahogany red with Rustin's clear plastic topcoat

With thanks to Andrew Guyton

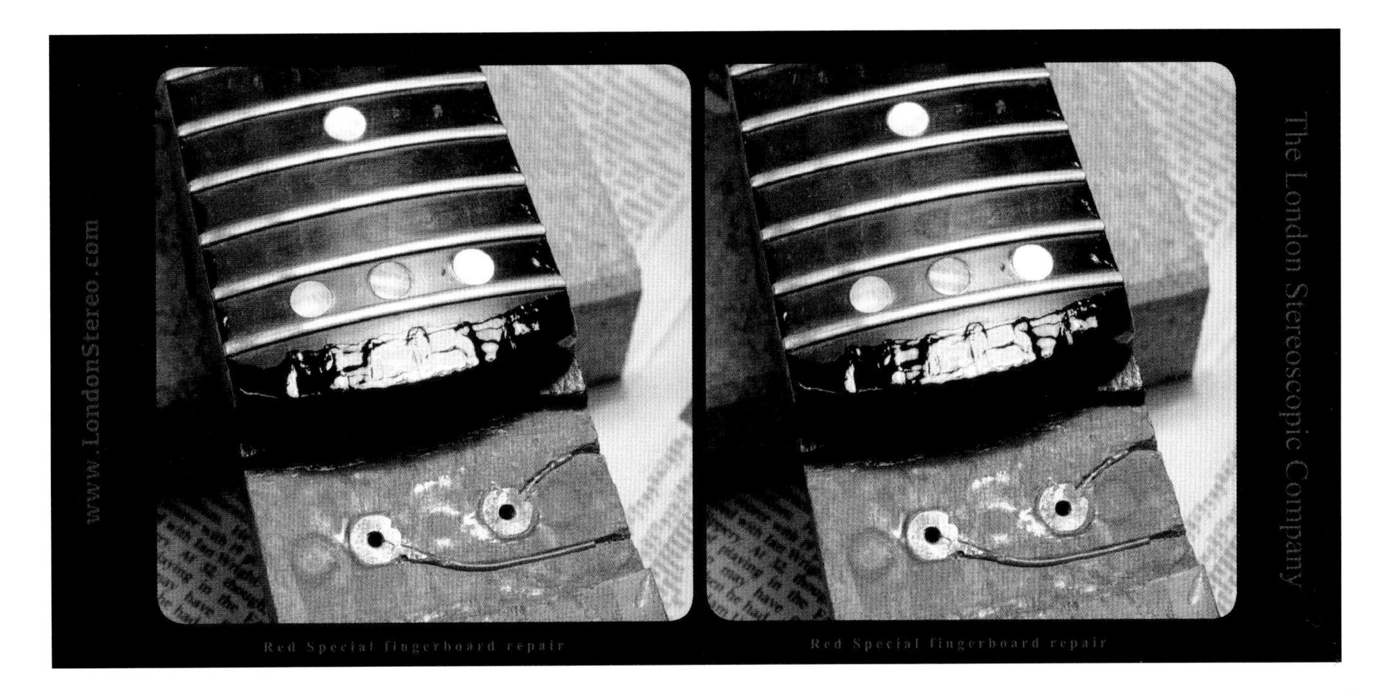

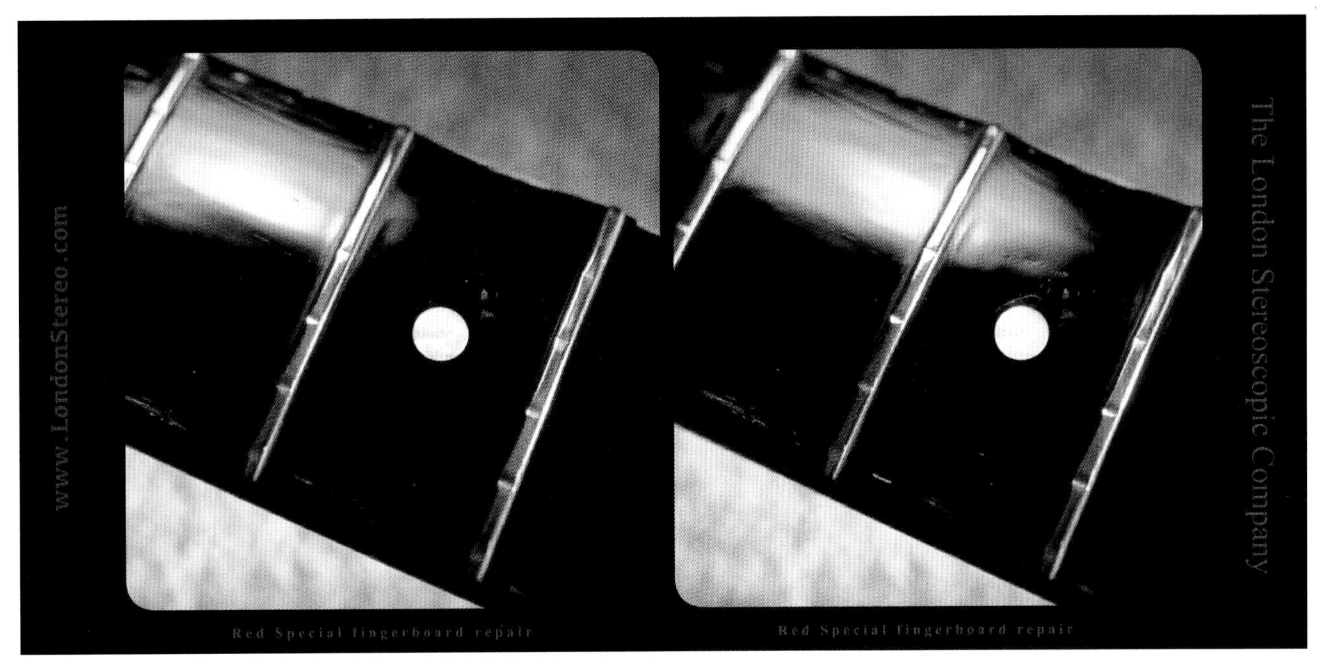

Top: "This picture of the end of the fingerboard being repaired 20 years later, shows the nuts which the screws holding the original pickups screwed into. They are buried in the wood of the neck, in Araldite, with the wires buried too, which link to the guitar circuit."

Above: A set of stereoscopic images that show not only the camber and shine of the fingerboard, but also the wear the frets have suffered over the years. Visit www.londonstereo.com, for more information on how best to view these images, plus much more.

Opposite: October 1964. Brian at home with the just finished Red Special, sitting next to a mahogany cupboard made by Harold May. At this stage the audience comprises just one member: Squeaky the cat, curled up in the foreground.

Opposite Below: "The [original] pickups had a wonderful bright sound," recalls Brian. "I'd plug into my Dad's home-made radio, by way of the input circuits on the preamp for our Collaro three-speed tape deck." Here, Brian is doing just that.

CHAPTER 4

THE QUEEN DAYS

Brian describes how the Red Special became part of the family, both on-stage and behind closed doors, as Queen evolved into one of the biggest bands of all time.

" I think everybody in Queen saw my Red Special guitar as part of the family; it was very much a part of our daily lives. Normally they didn't pick it up but I do remember – and I don't think I've ever told this story before – we were doing *A Kind Of Magic* with Dave Richards as producer. I was out of the studio – we were all in and out at different times, and it went on and on – and they'd got to the bit where the lyric is "I'm hearing secret harmonies". So Roger must have gone off and grabbed my guitar, plugged it into my amp and my system, and played that bit in the three-part harmony. I came back and I thought: "Hmmm..." because not only was it my guitar, but also I wouldn't have done it quite like that. So I always had that feeling that something had been slightly violated and it still feels strange. I'll do a kind of approximation to it if we're in concert, but I wouldn't have done it that way! "

I'm very proud of the fact that a lot of people have adopted the styles I evolved for harmony guitars and I always think it's a nice compliment. To me, harmony guitars aren't about just moving the first, third and fifth around up and down in parallel; that doesn't sound very good, really. To me, building up guitar harmonies is exactly like writing parts for an orchestra. The reason that works is that they're not moving in parallel but are moving in and out, making clashes, intertwining and making spaces: that, to me, is what writing arrangements is about.

One of the first things I remember learning in a group was that you can't stop playing. When you're at home on your sofa, you're trying something and it goes wrong, you stop and do it again. But if you're out there in front of an audience, there is no stopping and you have to find a way to deal with everything that goes wrong – that's a great education. There's a transition that takes place when you're in front of an audience, but if things go seriously wrong, you can't stop: that's what we learned and I kind of learned that all over again on tour with Kerry Ellis recently. It applies more to drummers than guitarists, though; if your drummer stops, you're dead!

Somebody said to me very early on, you can get away with anything in a group except for a bad drummer. It's true. You can get away with playing bad guitar or being a bad singer, but if the drummer's crap, forget it; people won't be able to jig along with it and will lose the plot. Luckily I've got a good drummer!

There was a lot to learn along the way to transform yourself from someone who plays in the living room to playing Wembley Stadium or whatever, so many things you have to get used to. Things like when you plug your lead in and if it's just hanging there, you'll tread on it and pull it out sooner or later, so you get used to winding it around the strap, simple things like that – but there are 500 more of them that can completely capsize you, if they go wrong.

You have to be very conscious of how you're treating the guitar so it stays in tune, which is difficult. I used to have problems in the beginning because it didn't stay in tune as well as I thought it would, especially in different temperatures, playing outdoors. Still one of the hardest things for me is playing in humid conditions. We played in Aruba with Paul Rodgers *[on October 8, 2005 – SB]* and it was like being covered in a wet blanket, my fingers went like sponges and I couldn't play the strings.

The guitar would suffer problems on occasion, though. It was flung about in flightcases and occasionally a wire would break. That would be a disaster because you'd have no way of knowing when that was going to happen, so we got used to taking it to bits regularly to check all the wiring to see if there were dry joints, and poke everything around to make sure it all still worked.

It's not a very easy place to be, being a Guitar Tech; if something goes wrong, it's your fault. I had Brian 'Jobby' Zellis with me for years and I know it was very stressful for him, especially when things would go wrong and I'd suddenly get no signal in the middle of a gig. He does something else now and I don't blame him. Pete *[Malandrone]* does it for me now and he has a very good temperament; you need to have that. He doesn't panic if something goes wrong and he has this system of back-up plans.

But in heat of battle you never know; anything can happen. I've played in almost every conceivable situation and the stress can be enormous if something goes wrong, as you don't have a safety net. So for me, and for Pete, it's a kind of learning curve you have to go on and you need to have the right temperament as well as the technical ability.

Losing the guitar was a worry and we got to the stage where whoever was working for me kept it with them at all times, or else it was locked up somewhere very safe. I don't know what I would do if it went. I have nice copies now, wonderful copies from *[luthiers]* Greg Fryer and Andrew Guyton that we use on the road and we have the stock Brian May Guitars issues now too, and I can use them. So, in theory, I could carry on if I lost the guitar but it would be a grave and terrible thing because it is like a part of me.

TECH TALK

"Brian has worked with three main Guitar Technicians during the most successful times and here, for the first time, each gives their personal recollections of life caring for the Red Special."

RICHIE ANDERSON, 1975–78

When did you start working with Brian?

I worked for Mott The Hoople and Queen toured with them a couple of times in late 1973/early 1974. We tried to help them out and make their equipment work better, and at one point they said I should call if I ever needed a job. In mid-1975 I did and they said "OK", and it was just as they were recording "Bohemian Rhapsody". I did three years then retired, and that's when Jobby took over.

What sort of regular maintenance did the guitar need on the road?

It really didn't need any maintenance apart from strings. For something that Brian and his Dad put together in the garden shed, it was really robust: they did a really good job of it. I think them both being scientists helped as they researched it and knew that the more solid the body was, the better it would be. I think the only problem I ever had was when it just stopped working at a soundcheck in Los Angeles; I opened it up and there was a tiny sliver of wire that had shorted something out.

What sort of security measures did you have for the guitar?

It lived in its own flight case so if it had got crushed it would probably have survived. As far as looking after it there was always somebody there keeping an eye on it and security was pretty good anyway. It was kind of ingrained in us, as people would try and nick stuff. Anything getting nicked could cause big problems but if the Red Special had gone… I used to think that Brian would be more concerned about security but he seemed to accept that we were a professional crew and that we'd look after it.

Are you aware of just how iconic the guitar is?

We were aware of the value of it and I knew he'd never use anything else. He was pretty tuned in to what he wanted, and it wasn't just the guitar but all the bits in between; which amp he was using, which speakers were in the amp, that sort of thing.

What spare guitars did you have?

He had this beige one *[made by John Birch – SB]* that he hated; it didn't sound the same. When he broke a string I'd have to get it changed and tuned back up as quickly as possible. He also had a Gibson Les Paul, which he used for one number, and a Yamaha acoustic that had a pickup in it.

What were they like to work for?

They were great. It's all been said before but Freddie wasn't the person you'd think he was; behind it all he was a very shy, nice guy. He was very ordinary in some ways and a complete other world from the showman.

What would you say was the best gig you saw Brian and Queen do?

They were great from the word go, but we didn't get to see much of that. When you're on the stage you're certainly not hearing or seeing it how the audience does. Also, if you're doing the job I was doing, you're looking all the time to see what's happening: maybe someone's chucked something, the guitar's stopped or a string's broken. But everyone knew they were going to be massive.

BRIAN 'JOBBY' ZELLIS, 1978–92

When did you start working with Brian?

I joined when they were doing the Jazz album in Montreux and the first gig I did with them was in Dallas in October 1978. *[Queen played Dallas Convention Centre on October 28, 1978 – SB]*

I'd always been into music and I was working for hire companies, doing all kinds of stuff. Someone told me that the position was available so I went and interviewed with Richie Anderson and the rest is history. I only ever planned to do a couple of tours with them and be on my way, but I stayed for over 14 years.

What sort of regular maintenance did the guitar need on the road?

I didn't really have the time to do serious work on it when on tour. Once it needed a new jack plug socket and fortunately we found one amongst Brian's Dad's old stuff; it probably came from the dash panel of a Spitfire or something! I'd keep the guitar clean and very occasionally there'd be a broken wire inside, but it really didn't need much in the way of maintenance.

Left: An elegantly flowing shot of Brian, the consummate guitar hero. Here he's strumming a prototype of what would become his first official signature model, the Guild BHM-1.

What sort of security measures did you have for the guitar?
Generally it'd travel with the rest of the equipment, which was pretty much the safest way to do it. If we were doing a radio show or something I'd have it under my bed, but in places like South America we'd lock it in the guitar trunk, hang that from the roof and have two guys with guard dogs sitting under it. There were times when I'd have a security guy with a gun follow me around: that 1981 tour was pretty wild!

Are you aware of just how iconic the guitar is?
I still have nightmares about losing the guitar, seriously. It's not like a Stradivarius where you can just go and buy another one: it's the Red Special, there isn't anything else like it.

What spare guitars did you have?
Originally it was the John Birch but he never liked that. Eventually he picked it up and a string went, so he chucked it over the back of the stage and it broke. *[This incident, substantiated by Brian, took place at the Brendon Burn Arena, The Meadowlands, New Jersey, August 9, 1982 – SB]*

What were they like to work for?
It certainly wasn't just a job but more like joining a family. Brian was brilliant to work with, like hanging out with your brother; if you had a problem and there was something he could do to fix it, he would.

What would you say was the best gig you saw Brian and Queen do?
They were absolutely incredible and on a good night, nobody compared. One of the problems I had was just getting caught up in the music: I'd be bopping away listening and someone would bang me on the head and tell me to go fix something.

PETE MALANDRONE, 1994–present

When did you start working with Brian?
I started working for Brian in January 1994, helping Justin Shirley-Smith put the studio together. Brian had a tech then who left to go and work for Blur, and I sort of took over. My first gig with him was when he guested on one song with Meat Loaf at the old Wembley Arena in December 1994.

What sort of regular maintenance does the guitar need on the road?
Regular maintenance is cleaning it. Brian's sweat is not very acidic: I've heard horror stories about people like Rory Gallagher where their sweat absolutely rots the guitar, but that's not the case with Brian. I'll just wipe the guitar down and check it; make sure it's not noisy, make sure the input jack's clean, that sort of thing. He doesn't really like the strings being changed but when I do change one I'll put Nut Sauce *[a specialised lubricant – SB]* on the nut and saddle rollers.

Do things go wrong with the guitar often?
We've had issues with the pots a couple of times and I've had a wire break off too, once just as he was about to do a "We Will Rock You" performance. The guitar just completely stopped working so he did it on a spare and when I took it apart, a wire had come off. They're 50-year-old wires and God knows how old they really are; I can't imagine they would have bought brand new wire when they were making it.

Are you aware of just how iconic the guitar is?
Absolutely. People ask me how I deal with that sort of responsibility and the only way I can do it is to not think about it: I try and treat it as if it's not what it is. If I was in any way apprehensive every time I touched it, or treated it with too much reverence, I wouldn't be able to work. Other guitar players who have had a go on it may be used to handling expensive instruments of their own but as soon you put Brian's guitar on them they change, and you can see it in their faces. I can't be like that if I've got to work with it.

What would you say was the best gig you've seen Brian and Queen do?
There are too many to mention, really. I get lost sometimes when he's playing really well, forget that I'm working and just sit there and watch. He played particularly well during the second gig at Hammersmith on the tour with Adam Lambert *[on July 12, 2012 – SB]*. It was a brilliant crowd too and I really enjoyed the gig. The MTV Awards he did with Lady GaGa too *[in Los Angeles on August 28, 2011 – SB]*; I really enjoyed that because it was a massive technical challenge and the audience was huge, and he just nailed that.

Above Right: The full bombast of Queen live in the U.S. in early 1977. The band toured the world constantly during this time, pausing only to write and record some of the greatest rock music ever.
Below Right: A wonderfully dynamic shot of Brian with Freddie Mercury in 1974. This was busy year for the band, with the release of *Queen II* and *Sheer Heart Attack*, plus numerous shows around the world, keeping the momentum going.

While the outfits, venue capacities, set-lists, production and even hair-lengths varied wildly over the years, the Red Special remained the only constant.

Brian on tour in the U.S., 1977. Queen played around 65 concerts over the course of two North American treks that year.

Above: An iconic shot from 1978. The circular red sticker that covers the hole in the scratchplate left by the Vox fuzz unit is clearly visible.

Overleaf: Brian, perched on his 'Vox Wall of Death' backline, Los Angeles, 1980. Brian's signal chain is deceptively simple but his tone is unmistakable.

VOX

VOX
VOX
VOX
sunn

Brian, Madison Square Garden, New York, September 30, 1980,
the final night of the US leg of *The Game* tour.

The *Crazy* tour has reached an almost mythic status amongst Queen aficionados. Here's Brian at the Manchester Apollo on November 27, 1979.

The Game U.S. tour, 1980. The band employed a lighting rig called the "Fly Swatters", replacing 1978/9's "Pizza Oven" design.

Above: The *Magic* tour included two shows at London's Wembley Stadium.
Here is the view from Brian's perspective from July 12, 1986.

Left: Brian on the Queen *Works!* tour, Europe, 1984. The *Metropolis* vibe and
eye-popping nature of the spectacular production still looms large in the memory.

Overleaf: Brian at Live Aid, Wembley Stadium, July 13, 1985. Queen hit the stage at
6.44pm and proceeded to blow the world away with a captivating performance.

Brian with Paul Rodgers, without doubt one of rock's greatest vocalists. He fronted Queen + Paul Rodgers for four years, both on tour and on the album *The Cosmos Rocks*.

Brian enjoyed surprising audiences at the Queen musical *We Will Rock You* with sporadic yet raucous appearances. The show, which stayed for 12 years at London's Dominion Theatre, closed on May 31, 2014 after 4,600 performances.

Brian performing at the closing ceremony of the 2012 Olympic Summer Games, Red Special in hand, gearing up to meet Roger Taylor and Jessie J for "We Will Rock You".

Adam Lambert has proved popular with Queen fans, not only for his incredible voice, but also his stage presence and persona. A huge American summer tour in 2014 was announced to much fanfare.

Brian with noted West End star Kerry Ellis, best known for show-stopping performances in both *We Will Rock You* and *Wicked*. The pair's "Acoustic By Candlelight" tours have proved immensely popular.

BEAT IT
PRETTY

CHAPTER 5

ON THE ROOF

Perhaps the most famous ever appearance of the Red Special happened on June 3, 2002, as part of the Party At The Palace concert celebrating Queen Elizabeth II's Golden Jubilee. This account of that ground-breaking moment atop Buckingham Palace roof was written by Brian immediately after the event when it was fresh in his mind. We reproduce it here in full for the first time...

"The true story of how I got to stand on that roof..."

It all started with my old friend, composer Michael Kamen, with whom I'd worked closely, making music for the film *Highlander* some years earlier. Michael phoned and asked me to go into the studio with him to put a guitar solo on his new Winter Olympics theme. He said casually, at the end of the phone conversation, "Oh, and I want to talk to you about something else too. The Palace want you to play at the Jubilee concert in June, and I think we could do something together…"

"Really? What would they like me to do?" I asked, a little incredulously. "They wondered if you would care to stroll through the state rooms of the Palace, playing the national anthem on solo guitar – Jimi Hendrix style," came the reply. I think the line went quite silent for a while. Then I caught my breath and said something like: "They can't be serious," and the conversation ended.

That night, I had a strange feeling that a 'moment' was in the offing, but could not imagine myself doing this thing. For a start, I had never played "God Save The Queen" live, as a solo piece or otherwise. I had recorded just one version in 1975, which was a multitracked arrangement for about 12 guitars. This version appeared on the Queen album *A Night At The Opera*, and the recording has been played at the end of virtually every Queen live show since that time. We actually tried running it at the end of our *We Will Rock You* musical, but somehow it didn't seem quite right at the time; now, it might be different, of course.

But to play this as a solo… strolling… hmmm… it didn't seem a possibility. Also, although Jimi Hendrix is still my greatest hero as a guitarist, I really don't play like him. I'm a different animal; my style is more structured, I don't have his 'chops', and I lack his wild 'Voodoo' genius. There was only one of him. Call me old-fashioned, but I thought if I was going to do something daring, it was going to be 'Brian May style', not a pastiche of someone else! I went to bed kind of upset, really.

Next morning, I had this crazy thought in my mind as I woke. The place to do such an insane thing was in the most insane place – not in the Palace, but up on the battlements, a lone piper, battered by wind and rain, performing as a symbol of rock's first 50 years, as if he had always been up there through the years of Queen Elizabeth's reign – and incidentally the entire span of my musical life. But such a thing had never been done. How adventurous would the Palace be?

Well, I rang Michael immediately, told him the idea, and asked him to run it by the organisers, fully expecting the answer to be: "Great idea, but sorry, it's not possible." The answer came back in no more than an hour. "They say 'okay'!"

So there it was. At that time the event was still months away, and I had enough on my mind leading up to the premiere of our beloved musical. Eventually, the first night came [WWRY *opened at London's Dominion Theatre on May 14, 2002*] and it went brilliantly, to a long, standing ovation. We had a blast, played at the party afterwards, and went home feeling that we had launched the ship. The only thing I had done in real terms to prepare for the Palace up to now was to order my costume – conversations with Tim Goodchild, designer of the brilliant *We Will Rock You* stage costumes, had culminated in a great design incorporating the titles of the best rock songs of the Jubilee years.

But now there was nothing in the way of the big shadow that was starting to loom. I looked this solo appearance in the face, with nothing between me and it. I had figured out that the solo piece could in fact be a kind of 'guitar voluntary', a short concerto for guitar and orchestra. I could hear it quite clearly in my head, but felt very worried because I only had a vague idea of how to bring it about.

It would start with a fanfare from the trumpets (the Queen's trumpets, I wondered?), which would set the stage for me, and would mean that I was getting a reliable signal that everything was working. Then an answering fanfare from me, the raucous yet 'brown' sound of a huge guitar chord from my old instrument, followed by an improvised ascending figure like I had used in some of the old Queen solos in our live show, when I used two repeats to build harmonies. Perhaps I would use these delay machines to give that huge harmony effect here? Yes, this would not be at all like Mr Hendrix: it would be very diatonic, closer to my original roots, and Queen's. I love the blues, but for me, it is a cloak to slip in and out of according to mood, and this was not a blues moment. Then there would be the tune proper, "God Save The Queen", done very much in the style of the top line of my 'opera' version, but supported not by more guitars but by full orchestra, mainly strings to begin with, to keep it smooth and poignant. Then, when the endnote came, where would it go? On the 1975 version it crossed over sweetly to the sub-dominant chord with a rather mournful little cadence winding back up to the resolving G chord: there seems to be tradition of doing this tune in G, and to my ears it can't be bettered.

So this time? Not small, but a big ending was what I wanted. I could hear a descending snaking sequence of guitar, *à la* the "Bo Rhap" solo, over an ascending orchestral C chord; then, not a quiet return to the tonic, but an attacking rising guitar figure over a more dangerous E♭ major, the other choice of chord containing the tonic G note, the orchestra in holding pattern, and then a final rising guitar attack in the home G major, culminating in three huge whacks of synchronised all-out guitar and all-out orchestra.

This was the theory in my head. As soon as there was a moment, I went in to join Justin [Shirley-Smith] and Kris [Fredriksson], my studio chaps, who were in Sphere Studios mixing *Queen Greatest Hits* in DTS surround. I had a listen to what they were doing, made a few comments, and then settled down in front of the computer, and in about four hours, more or less without looking up, I sketched out the format of the arrangement using orchestra samples. I based it loosely on the skeleton of the 1975 version for the feel of the middle section, but then replaced everything with orchestra, so the old guitar version was no longer needed. It then took about half an hour to put a guide guitar on – very imperfect, but I enjoy this bit. Suddenly, it sounded like it might just work. Justin thought so; always a good sign, since he doesn't easily get impressed!

I took the demo home, suddenly feeling much better, for now I had a definite plan. I played it to Anita and she loved it, so I now settled down to take it to the next stage. I went round to Mr Kamen's place to talk orchestra stuff. Now, I'm fine at getting my thoughts into demo orchestra form, but not capable of converting this into dots for a bunch of orchestra players to read! Michael was overloaded, and so was his right-hand man James Brett, so we agreed we would get another chap to do the transcription. I would be able to check it in three days' time, and then there would be three more days before the live show. The organisers and Michael strongly suggested recording a 'backup' tape of the song, just in case it would not be possible to get it together live on the day. I agreed, since it was also going to give me an opportunity to try it out live with the orchestra. But I had no intention of using the tape on the day – for me, the whole point was that this was to be a symbol of live, real alive music.

I was busy until the day the orchestration came back, but the roof was now always in the back of my mind. Would it work?

Above: Brian, from the arena stage, points out the location of the roof plinth to Ben Elton, a noted creative force and writer of the book of the musical *We Will Rock You*, and to Tony Vincent, *WWRY*'s first Galileo.

Would the orchestra and I be able to negotiate our way through the pauses and changes of pace?

The evening came when the orchestration arrived. It came as a computer file in a program format known as Sibelius. My computer didn't know this format, but Michael's did. We were able to zoom into any part of the arrangement and immediately hear it, again in synthesised form, but now formalised in a manner that would be readable by, say, the first violin, the timpani player, or the trumpets. It was pretty good; some little errors which we could correct on the spot, but on the whole, close to what I had asked for.

So the next day found me in the beautiful, huge tracking room in the new Air Studios. Some of the other artists were also there: Annie Lennox, rehearsing her fabulous version of "Sisters", the enormously talented Phil Collins, who was to drum on practically everything throughout the Jubilee night, and the rest of the incredibly high-level 'house band' – the legendary Steve Winwood, Phil Palmer, Pino Palladino, and Ray Cooper, that incomparable percussionist – my God, what a line-up!

And the orchestra was there, too. I had expected a bunch of middle-aged men looking at their watches and rather looking down on the 'rock' proceedings. But here was a team of bright, enthusiastic young men and women, giving it every bit of effort they had in their bodies. What a joy! They were from the London Royal Academy of Music, and a finer group of young professionals I had never before encountered.

Now I had to deliver. There was little point in trying to rehearse or record my piece without the guitar, because the whole point was that the piece was interactive. This was to be a steep learning curve for us all, but especially me! Michael was very tired after many long days on the project, and I didn't want to try anyone's patience.

Well, I'd love to tell you it all fell into place right away, but it didn't. We rolled the tape and did probably a dozen takes, but every one was flawed. Either I did something unpredictable, or Michael was unable to bring the orchestra back in with me, or some other problem occurred. I began to get very sweaty, conscious that my intonation, and certainly reproducibility, was far inferior to that of the orchestra players. I felt very foolish, especially as this was my piece, and it was starting to seem as if

Above: The calm before the storm. A shot taken from Brian's vantage point on Buckingham Palace's roof, showing the empty arena during soundcheck. He's just visible on the two huge screens flanking the stage.

I had written something that was impossible to play. I had tried to leave the scheme with room in it for me to play more or less what I wanted in the flourishes. But this almost by definition meant that Michael would not be able to sense when the orchestra needed to restart, until it was too late. And if we couldn't get it right in a nice warm studio, when we could all see each other, how on earth would it ever work in the wildly inhospitable conditions of trying to play it with me on a roof and the orchestra in a garden 500 metres away? It was a humiliating moment for me. We sent the orchestra off with thanks, and apologies from me for messing them about.

Then Justin and Giles Martin, son of the excellent George Martin, sat with me for what seemed like an eternity, trying to cobble together a useful 'best of' tape to use as our fail-safe plan. The trouble was, I was beginning to see that in reality, there could be no safe backup plan. How could I possibly go up there and mime after all this? Our manager Jim Beach then phoned and came over, having been to the Dominion to see a performance of our *WWRY* show that I had missed because of this struggle. I told him I was in trouble. He arrived, and enthused hugely about the take we had put together. He had not heard my demo, and he now said he thought the concept, and the sound of our demo, was magnificent. "But", he said, "Brian, don't put yourself into an impossible situation – you cannot count on pulling this off live on a roof." At this point, everyone seemed to agree, and the great Ray Cooper, who had kindly stayed on to lend his support, offered to put some percussion on, live on the night. I was thrilled, but hang on – so the percussion would be live on the night but I wouldn't? Ouch – too awful to contemplate.

I went home almost convinced by everyone that it would be all right on the night somehow. I played it to Anita, and she was very excited. She said, "So what's the problem?" I told her that the real problem was that I was an unpredictable quantity, and there was a 90 per cent chance that I was going to let everybody down: the organisers, the Palace audience, two billion TV viewers, Queen, *the* Queen, and myself.

She said, "Well, you'll have to practise!" I got very edgy at this suggestion. For years, I have found that I have to leave a certain amount to improvise on the night, or I feel stiff and uncreative. But I was to learn a new lesson. I sat there and contemplated

Above: The audience inside the Palace Grounds numbered 12,000 with thousands more crammed into The Mall, all soaking up the spectacle. Performers included Sir Paul McCartney, Eric Clapton and Joe Cocker.

HOTEL

two impossibilities. I was not able to guarantee getting it right live, and when I tried to mime it in my living room, I realised I wasn't capable of pulling that off either, because I really do play stuff differently every time. I knew I would look stupid trying to pretend; my fingers would be in the wrong place. So there was apparently no way forward. I went to bed in total despair, and prayed for a solution, admitting complete powerlessness, like a good human being in 'recovery'!

In the morning – this is now the Saturday before the show, mercifully a rare free day – and I am ashamed to say I spent most of it in semi-paralysis, not wanting to face the fear of failure. However, when I eventually got myself together, I just sat down and played the two versions I had on the CDR over and over again, one with guitar, and one without, and yes, practised. And it worked. After about five hours, on and off for cups of tea, I had taught myself a way of playing the piece that was reproducible, decipherable by the orchestra, and that I could get right 90 per cent of the time. I now convinced myself that I could do both things instead of neither. I could play it live, and if conditions forbade that, I could mime it decently. Still that revulsion about miming remained, but now I had my self-control back; I was no longer afraid to face it. Still afraid of screwing up, but not too afraid to give it a shot.

I called up James, Michael, Giles and Justin, and told them all this. We agreed we would make a decision at 2pm on the day of

BUCK HOUSE BLAZES

PRACTICE: Brian May

FLAMING HELL: Fire engines race to Buckingham Palace as smoke pours from the roof

Top: Team May on the roof plinth, with the Palace grounds in the background. Left to right, guitar tech Pete Malandrone, Brian, his personal assistant Sara Bricusse and manager Jim Beach.

Above Right: How the press reported the fire at the Palace which nearly scuppered the whole shebang. "It looked serious for a while," Brian remembers, "as the army appeared and I was told to be careful; I might be shot if I stepped off the lawn! But they sorted it pretty quickly."

Left: Brian at soundcheck, striking the pose that would sum up the entire event in the press coverage to follow. For the Red Special, it was business as usual …

show, when we first got the chance to try it out.

But I insisted that we try it live first – that I get my shot, and if it works, I get to do it for real.

The next day was rehearsal day at the Palace proper for the first time. Just looking at the roof as we drove up gave me the horrors, but we had a nice day, rehearsing "Bohemian Rhapsody" and our other tunes with the great cast of our musical, *We Will Rock You*, and enjoying the beautiful gardens in the sunshine – what a treat to be in such a privileged and private place. But I was not able to go on the roof and try out my gear just yet. That was scheduled for tomorrow. I stayed behind late to rehearse with Joe Cocker, but then the notorius fire broke out, and we were evacuated to the region of the tennis courts, as was documented in the papers. I did an impromptu mobile phone interview for some radio station and apparently I was quoted as saying, "I can see a large bunch of very famous people milling about on a small piece of grass, waiting to find out what will happen next." It looked serious for a while, as the army appeared and I was told to be careful – I might be shot if I stepped off the lawn! But they sorted it pretty quickly. Of course, there was now a doubt about whether we would be able to go on the roof tomorrow, after such an event. After all, there were five tons of fireworks not far from where the fire broke out. I did the rehearsal stuff with Joe, always a pleasure, and went home wondering if my big decision would now be taken away from me. More practising at home!

Now cut to the morning of the show. I go in early, to rehearse with Cliff Richard. Now this is another treat for me – in fact, a childhood dream come true. Cliff was a huge star when I was a kid, and my Dad and I used to play his songs at home when I was learning the guitar as a boy. Now I get to play this man's first hit, a real rocker of the day called "Move It". It's very cool for me. I am called on to play in a style close to where I started in my quest for my own style – it's the beginnings of 'squeezing' notes across the fingerboard to raise the pitch, string bending – a journey which eventually enabled the likes of Clapton and Hendrix to use the guitar much more like a violin than the rhythm instrument it had hitherto been. In this song, in 2002, I have to play in a way

Above Right: A plainly nervous yet focused Brian mere minutes away from probably the most famous, and risky, performance of his life.

Above Left: The stage for 1986's *Magic* Tour was 20m (64ft) long. As Brian gets the pose just right, it's obvious that the plinth is more modest in size.

that makes it look much more difficult to bend the strings than is usual these days – the pioneers used thick, unyielding strings, not like the thin wiry ones I have, which allow me to bend up, and stay there as long as I want. I enjoy the experience, especially as S Club Seven are also involved, and a couple of them are very pretty indeed! They're also very professional and Cliff has taught them a new arrangement in a very short time, which they deliver very impressively.

In the back of my mind? The hour is approaching… I glance up at the chosen tower and I can see people working up there, preparing my guillotine, or so it seems! And now rain clouds are gathering. A few spots of rain start to fall. It gets gloomy, or is it just me?

My designated time for my soundcheck on the roof is 2pm. But the hour arrives, and they are not ready. I'm getting very edgy. The atmosphere backstage in the elegant tents they have provided for us is relaxed. Everyone here is a professional – everyone has worked hard to make the most of their spot. Most of these people are the absolute cream of our profession and it gives me a glow just to look around and know that I am with them, sharing this new adventure. There's a little table over there with an illustrious group, snacking in the uncertain light. Bryan Adams is there, with Eric Clapton, Ray Cooper, and my friend Michael Kamen. I'm a little shy of pushing myself in there as they probably have important things to discuss, but Eric catches my eye with a friendly wave, and a "Hi Brian", so I go over and chat. Eric is always kind and generous to me. I still hold him in such awe that it makes it a little difficult for me to talk to him. Intrigued by the roof thing, he says, "You're braver than I am – I wouldn't do it!" I say I'm damn sure he would do it better than me. He smiles modestly, and shakes his head, and says, "But apparently they can't do it live, right?"

My heart goes cold. So 'they' – some folks – have decided this without me? I ask Michael, but he says he needs to talk to the technical people again. At this point, I think I became gripped in a wave of angst, and headed off to find someone to shout at. They promised me my shot! I think I remember Sara *[Bricusse, Brian's personal assistant]* calming me down and, eventually, a little buggy arrives to take me to the spot on the Palace patio, from where I will be escorted to the roof. It's now around three. Up we go, a little band of adventurers, but I feel lonely and small, not a hero at all. In the end, I will be facing this test alone.

We get up there, and, well, nothing is working quite right yet. It's actually hard to judge what it should sound like, because there's quite a wind, but at least it has stopped raining. Some people are asking me what I will do if it pours with rain. I answer in a jolly way: "It'll be fine – Freddie will see to that!" Funny thing is, I believe it. Everybody laughs nervously.

I start to play the guitar, turning up the amplifiers, edging up onto my four by four foot plinth, and something goes very wrong. It had seemed a bit quiet, but now the sound farts and disappears. Pete Malandrone pulls a wry face and disappears into the bowels of my gear. I have by now decided to ditch all the effects I was going to use: no harmonisers, no delays. I had found that clarity was the most effective, so each note will be equally carried by the three Vox AC30s in perfect synch, but with a slight chorus effect which should make it sound enormously thick. Just me and a guitar and a lot of amplification, really. No props. Well, at the moment, no guitar noise at all! There is one other problem – the foldback monitors from the stage is not working. This was my worst nightmare. There will be no way of hearing the orchestra at all, except delayed by almost a second. I start to freak out. I begin to say to everyone, "Look, this simply will not be possible – you'd better start telling people..."

My stomach is in a knot, and I feel really unhappy. But now Pete reappears. "There was a faulty connection," he declares. "That's why the amps seemed quiet." I cluck at the strings – yes! – a nice fat cluck comes back at me. Real power! I start to feel energised. But now I look down into the gardens, and it's getting very crowded down there. They are letting the audience in. They are cheering and waving in little groups, obviously thinking all is well and I'm having a great time. Now I see my own family waving up at me. I give them a jolly wave, and a slight shrug, I think. I hope they are enjoying the moment.

My talkback to the stage has not materialised either, and the video screen is the size of a postage stamp and impossible to see in the daylight. I can only communicate with the technicians down below via a man with a walkie-talkie radio. It feels like being behind enemy lines! I ask him: "What the hell's happening with my monitors?" The huge speakers are there, but they are silent. No foldback, no hint of an orchestra, although I can distantly hear the strains of them playing my song on the wind, sounding a million miles away. They might as well be.

"No, we can't fix it yet," he says. "Security won't let the guy up with a replacement wire!" Great. It's four o'clock, and I really could do with being somewhere else.

Suddenly, there's a splutter from the speakers. It comes and goes, but I can now hear the tape I had practised to a hundred times or more. I jump up on the dais half way through the song

Below Left: On the buggy after the performance. The team's relief and joy is plain to see, as is the emotion behind Brian's clenched fist.

Below Right: Brian, seen from the audience below. His concerns that he wouldn't live up to his customary high standards proved unfounded.

and start to play. Miracle of miracles, I can hear everything. It's all deafening, huge and crisp, very exciting, and I can hear my guitar, and I can hear the orchestra, and I know in a sudden rush: I can do this. The thing finishes, the small crowd down below cheers, and I step down to talk to the linkman. I say, "I can do this – it's good enough." He hesitates, frowns, and says, "They are saying down there that we have go for playback. The synchronisation is going to be out otherwise." "No it isn't", I shout, probably with the odd expletive. "We agreed that I get my shot at doing it live, and then we make our decision. I get my promised one run at it." "Well right now the orchestra is on a break, so we can only run it to tape." "Then so be it. I will play to that for now, but you guys run it now, and we'll see if I can do it, and if it is in synch." They say yes. The clicks thump out – it's ear splitting up here, just with one snare drum! Then the fanfare, then I go for it. All the way. It all sounds great; I feel confidence and power surging through me. We get to the end, and without a hitch. Check the truck… They say "okay". Check out front… They say "okay". I say, "Run it again, and we will know if that was a fluke or not." We run it, it goes great, and I feel my strength growing. I can f***ing do this!

Silence. So? How does it sound? The word comes back. "Great, it's sounding better all the time – possibly better than the demo." I say, "Guys, we are doing this. I am doing this live. There is no going back. I am not an actor, I am a player – if I wake up tomorrow morning and I have walked away from this once-in-a-lifetime opportunity to do this thing for real, I will never be able to live with myself." They all nod... and the die is cast.

We go down, getting hopelessly lost in the Palace in the process – but that's another story entirely – and we're all a bit hysterical now. It would be nice to have a beer, but I choose not to as I want to be perfectly clear and in control of my senses. Just a few hours to wait...

At 6:45, we trundled up again, to do the thing. I have had time for the elation to die away now, and I just felt kind of dark and broody, but focused. Fear was just outside the door, barking furiously. But I had a slight detachment. "Play me some click," I said to the walkie-talkie man. "I have to know I will hear it." A pause. They did it. At that point, I didn't know what I was going to hear in the monitors, the recorded orchestra or the real one. At that point I didn't care. After all my rehearsals, I felt I could

Above: Buckingham Palace, London, June 3, 2002. The full scale of the live arena's production. Brian draws a crowd even when soundchecking.

deal with whatever came along. Pete stepped up on to the dais to check everything was audible, to huge cheers from below! He steps down, hands me the guitar, and now we wait. 7:20pm – "10 minutes, Brian." "Five minutes, Brian." Then, "One minute to the lead-in link."

Silence, then the clicks, the snare drum and, finally, the mighty fanfare from the trumpets. I am feeding back, a nice growing, singing note, building up and up in intensity. I'm ready with the pick, an old sixpence with a nice serrated edge for that metallic edge. Then I'm in. I hit the big D chord, and it sounds crunching and massive. I feel joy, hope, history, and it feels like a long road ahead, though it's actually only one minute 50 seconds! Jeff Posner, the director, had persuaded me to cut out the first C chord sequence at the end because of the tight time constraints; I think it actually improved it. A big run up the fingerboard to a held scream; I know exactly how long I can scream now. A moment of air. Now, the fragile tranquillity of the tune proper. Only a finger is used to pluck these notes; the pick makes them too harsh. Any slight slip will be most apparent here – everybody knows how this tune sould go! Now the deceptively tricky little twiddly bit that takes me into the second half of the tune. Don't rush it. And now I am negotiating the steps up that bring me into the "...send her victorious..." bit in a higher octave – every note is screaming now. And an error of a fraction of an inch on either hand may cause the vibration of that thin little string to stop and I will have egg on my face. One note actually does almost die a little, but it's all within the limits of 'live and dangerous'. I am feeling full of glorious passionate love for those high squeezed notes. They are singing to me, pulling themselves into tune. This is somehow the moment I dreamed of since I was a kid. The extra adrenaline really seems to wring out every drop of passion from my body. Now I'm at the last note of the melody, the start of my descending cadence. It flicks off the fingers quite nicely, if a little more tersely than the rehearsal.

Now the long wait, the moment of the breath before the final onslaught. A great thrash on an open G, and the last aggressive run up to my repeated 'classic' false ending, an alternating pair of chords over and over again – it occurs to me at this point I never counted them – this is one bit I didn't fully peg down. I'm glad. Now, the final gap, and three chords remain. Am I home? One – crash. Two – crash. And...

The final, gigantic thrash. It lasts forever, at least an hour in my perception. I can see it travelling down my wire, into the amp, out of the speakers, into the microphones, down the cable to the mixing desk, out into the speakers in the garden, into the huge systems in the Mall, in Green Park, in St James's Park, and

Top: The moment a photographer captures the image that would grace the pages of many a newspaper in the days to come.

Above: Brian showing off the Union Jack lining of the costume created by Tim Goodchild, who also designed the *We Will Rock You* stage outfits.

Right: The view from The Mall as Brian takes off the Red Special, safe in the knowledge that the performance far exceeded expectations.

into the air towards televisions all around the globe. Finally to millions who, thanks be to God, have now had it all the way it was meant to be. It was done.

I pulled off the guitar and pushed it in the air, and screamed my gratitude to the Great Spirit above my head. I think the cameras had left me by then… and life started all over again. I was the other side of the wall. My final satisfaction was when I learned the orchestra had played live with me. Michael Kamen had brilliantly conducted them to be in synch with our back-up version, which was the one I was synching to. So the world heard our complete live take after all, held to a shape we were all familiar with.

To sum up… I was thrilled that "God Save The Queen" on the roof came out so well. It was the closest to jumping off a cliff without a parachute that I have come! It's strange; I think you might imagine that these days, with all the electronic apparatus that's available, maybe I could have invoked some helpful box to enable the solo piece to be easier for me. I can assure you that no such device exists! It was, at 7:29pm on that cold turret on the roof, Bri's Tower, just me and a guitar and a crouching cameraman. Pete, Sara and a handful of technicians were a little way away, offering up prayers!

For the 48 hours leading up to that moment, all I could think of were all the things that could make it go wrong – wind, cold hands, rain, inability to hear the orchestra, or hearing them with a delay, amplifier problems, strings breaking, high nerves leading to a silly mistake, tuning problems, orchestra hesitation or over-enthusiasm, slipping backwards off my platform, a faulty lead, slippery or sore fingers, or just plain ineptitude! I offered up a big prayer to the Great Spirit that I would not screw up!

Thankfully, my prayer was answered; none of the above happened, and I will never forget that incredible feeling rushing through my body as I launched into the fanfare, the energy driving my fingers against the tension of the strings to make the pushed notes, the hours it seemed to take until I piloted myself through the well-known central tune to the final flourish, and the elation and almost disbelief as I hammered the last three chords, knowing 'it was done'. For the first time in history, as my son put it, "A bloke had stood atop the first building in the land and made a big noise with a guitar" – an act unthinkable at the beginning of the present monarch's reign. I am immensely proud that I could make it happen.

I had written the arrangement with a respect both for Her Majesty and the office of the throne, and for the heritage of rock music, which, in a sense, gave me birth and took me to this place. I felt I was doing it for every kid who ever picked up

Above: Says Pete Malandrone, "Once he'd played it, I was the first one up… to grab the guitar. I could see the relief in his face and we had a big, proper hug."

Above Right: Performing 'We Are The Champions' with singer Will Young, supported by Roger Taylor, Phil Collins and the cast of *We Will Rock You*.

Right: Brian with Cliff Richard, fulfilling a childhood dream. "He was a huge star when I was a kid, and my Dad and I used to play his songs at home."

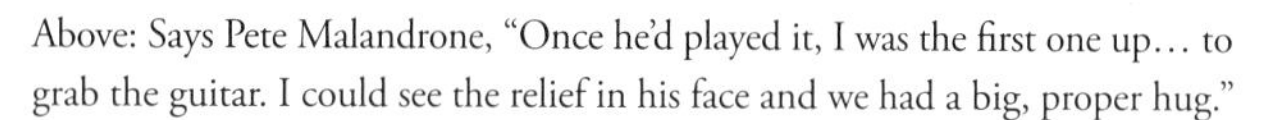

a guitar and felt the urge to conquer the world! I'm hoping that, maybe, my arrangement will be taken up by future performers at a royal occasion!

The next day, almost every newspaper carried a picture of that moment on the front page. Some of them thought the arrangement was 'bizarre'. Strange; I remember the day they broadcast the live version of "All You Need Is Love". It sounded bizarre at first, but later, it became quite cosy and accessible. I think this will too; after a couple of listens on the CD when it comes out, it will be apparent that what I did contained strong traditional influences. They had just never been put together with a rock guitar in the lead role before.

My outfit that day was designed by Tim Goodchild, in response to me commissioning him to create a look that would symbolise the spirit of the last 50 years of rock, or the first 50 years, if you like. Which correspond exactly with the 50 years of Queen Elizabeth's reign too.

It was specially made by a Savile Row tailor, with fabric printed by Joy Bondini and Nicola Killeen, both also part of our show team at the Dominion. The trousers were, at my request, an echo of the bohemian gear worn by Luke in the show. They are an amazing collage of fabrics and mechanical oddments. The waistcoat and shirt were created to tie the whole thing together, and the complete outfit was 'distressed' to make it look as if it, and I, had been standing up on that roof in all weathers for the last 50 years. Even the trainers were distressed! It's not in my handwriting, but I gave them a list of songs to incorporate in various fonts. I don't know if it was apparent from the TV shots, but the jacket has a lining of a large, faded, Union Jack.

As for that moment of delivery, I shared it with my friend, conductor and composer Michael Kamen, way down below in the Palace Gardens, and his superb young orchestra of handpicked students from the Royal Academy of Music; again, what fine young talents they are! They eventually gave me a bigger TV monitor up there on the roof to establish visual contact, but on the night it didn't work, because the light was too bright reflecting off the screen, so I had to rely only on the sound, and 'feel'.

The final fairy dust was provided by the superb Ray Cooper,

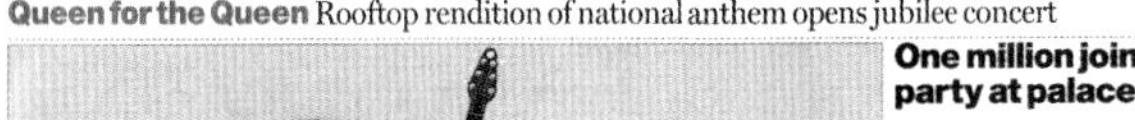

Queen for the Queen Rooftop rendition of national anthem opens jubilee concert

One million join party at palace

Rebecca Allison, Jack Bellamy and Stephen Bates

Twelve thousand pairs of eyes gazed skywards at the lone figure of Queen guitarist Brian May stood on the roof of Buckingham Palace and launched into a surreal performance of the national anthem.

The long-awaited Party in the Palace had begun and performers and crowds were embarked on a musical odyssey through the past 50 years.

It marked the culmination of a day in which guns were fired in salute from Hyde Park to Edinburgh, hundreds of street parties were held and the nation was encouraged to take part in a mass singing of the 1967 Beatles' hit All You Need is Love.

An estimated one million people packed the grounds of Buckingham Palace and the royal parks to witness the Queen light the final golden jubilee beacon in a chain stretching around the world and trigger a spectacular display of fireworks at the palace.

The Queen arrived for the pop concert with the Duke of Edinburgh with half an hour to go and was introduced by Dame Edna Everage as the "golden jubilee girl".

The royal couple, more at home with classical music, were in time to see Eric Clapton play Layla, although the Queen appeared to be wearing yellow ear plugs.

Other members of the royal family arrived in time for the opening performances and joined Tony and Cherie Blair in a VIP box. Among them were Prince Andrew and daughters Beatrice and Eugenie, Prince Edward and his wife Sophie, Princess Anne, Prince Charles, Prince Harry and Prince William, who elicited a hysterical response from some quarters.

The 12,000 fans who succeeded in a telephone ballot for tickets for last night's extravaganza had already enjoyed a jubilee picnic in the palace gardens as they watched the build-up to the concert.

Afterwards Prince Charles said: "Your Majesty ... Mummy. Ladies and gentlemen, in my long experience of pop concerts, this has been something very special indeed.

"I don't think that any of us will ever forget this evening. It really has been a wonderful celebration of some of the best of British musical talent. Well, nearly all British. And when you're talking about British talent, my goodness, there's a lot of it about."

Today will see the final day of the jubilee celebrations, involving a royal procession and thanksgiving service at St Paul's cathedral culminate in a fly-past over Buckingham Palace involving Concorde and the Red Arrows display team.

Jubilee reports, pages 4–5
Royal poem, G2, page 6

who'd offered to give me a boost by playing percussion; and our own Roger Taylor, who added extra timpani rolls in his own unique style to give the moment the final polish. After my moment of exhilarated thanks to the heavens, it was off down to the main stage to prepare for the main Queen set.

Now back to reality. My car wouldn't start the next morning! I faced it with a smile.

TECHNICAL FOOTNOTES

Guitar Tech Pete Malandrone was also part of Brian's momentous performance. Here he gives his unique insight into the day.

"It was terrifying. What happened was they craned the gear up there a couple of days before, but I wasn't allowed up to the roof until the actual day because I didn't have the right security clearance. Also, it rained a lot and I had to trust that it was covered up and that it would work. It worked fine when I fired it all up, but then just before Brian was about to play, it suddenly sounded terrible. There was a BBC sound guy crouched behind where I was and a cameraman, all in the tiny gap behind the gear and one of them had half-pulled a jack out of the rack. So, I looked, but I couldn't see it as it was so dark in the back there. I just pushed everything in and that did it.

"Once I'd fixed that, I knew there was nothing more I could do; if he broke a string, there wouldn't be enough time to change it, if the power went off there was nothing I could do about that, there was nothing more I could do for him so I felt powerless, and that's when the nerves really came. Once I knew my bit was all right, my nerves were for him as I knew how nervous he was and I just prayed that nothing untoward happened, as I knew how much it meant to him. Once he'd played it, I was the first one up on the rostrum to grab the guitar, I could see the relief in his face and we had a big, proper hug."

Above and Left: Just two of the national newspapers to feature Brian front and centre. "I was thrilled that 'God Save the Queen' on the roof came out so well. It was the closest to jumping off a cliff without a parachute that I have come!"

Overleaf: The true precariousness of standing alone on the roof of Buckingham Palace, totally live in front of a TV audience of hundreds of millions, Red Special in hand and fire in heart. It's unlikely that anything quite like this will happen again.

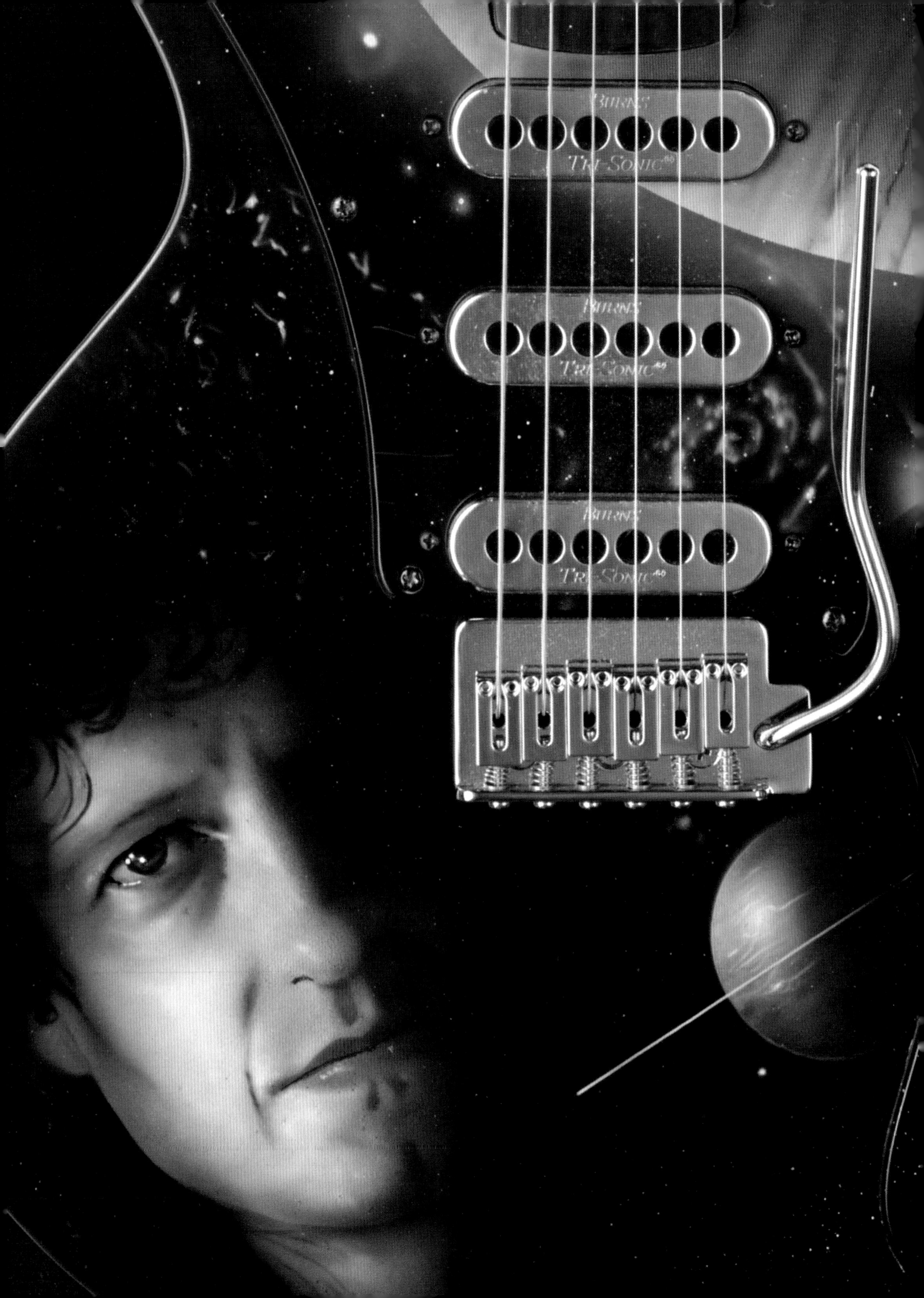
Burns
Tri-Sonic
Burns
Tri-Sonic
Burns
Tri-Sonic

CHAPTER 6

RED SPECIAL IN PRODUCTION

The Red Special has inspired countless guitar builders to try their hand at recreating what Brian and his father created. This final chapter highlights a selected history of instruments that have been manufactured using the Red Special as a direct influence. Some are widely available to buy whilst others are significantly rarer, and all come from Brian's personal collection.

BMG 3-TONE SUNBURST

One of the many finish options available throughout the Brian May Guitars range.

BMG ANTIQUE CHERRY

This lovely cherry finish is close to the colour of the Red Special itself.

BMG BASS

A relatively new venture, the result of much careful development, this one is already proving very popular with bass players. All BMG models have been overseen by both Brian and House Music in London.

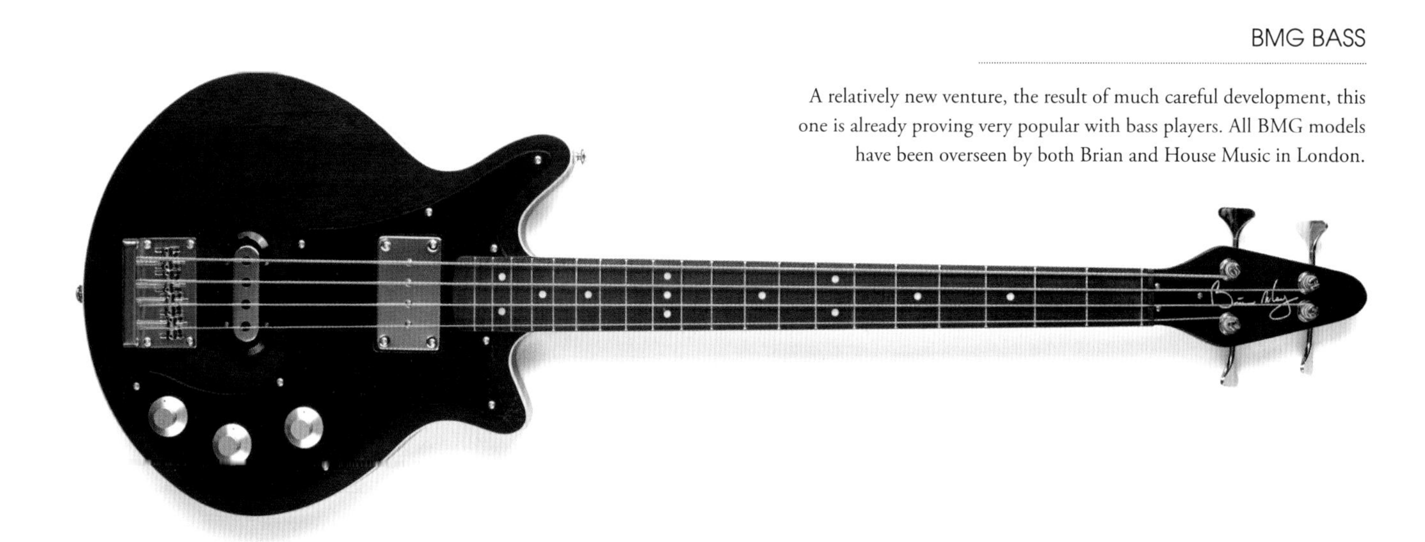

BMG ANATO PROTOTYPE

A vital part of producing quality guitars for commercial purposes is the process of building proof-of-concept and prototype instruments. This one-off, featuring the iconic *A Night At The Opera* sleeve design, is a good example of that and, up close, it's stunning.

BMG "FACE"

A 60th birthday present to Brian from Barry Moorhouse of House Music, the man who, with Brian and Pete Malandrone, launched Brian May Guitars in 2004. Barry commissioned Paul Karslake, British artist and the brother of Jo Wood (former wife of Rolling Stone Ronnie Wood), to create the unique finish.

BMG BLACK GOLD

Boasting gold-plated parts and a moody black finish, this version is amongst the coolest of all BMG models.

BMG HONEY SUNBURST

The unmistakable lines of the guitar suit this classic 'burst finish perfectly. Sheer class.

BMG MINI MAY

A travel or junior version of the Old Lady equipped with a single Tri-Sonic and a 17-inch scale.

BMG NATURAL

A natural finish that shows off the grain of the mahogany beautifully.

BMG THE RHAPSODY

An acoustic inspired by the Red Special, in a natural gloss finish. Despite its modest dimensions, there's no shortage of tone.

BMG UKULELE PROTOTYPE

Returning to where it all started; the perfect fusion of Uke and Red Special, for those Leroy Brown moments.

BMG SILVER

A new finish for the range: silver sparkle. Each BMG guitar follows the specification of the Red Special as closely as commerciality will allow, with features including an acoustic pocket hidden within the mahogany body, a trio of Burns Tri-Sonic pickups and, of course, an identical switching system.

BURNS EMILY

This is the only pink Burns Brian May Signature in existence, custom-finished for Brian's daughter Emily.

BMG VISION PROTOTYPE

A rare public glimpse of a true prototype, this BMG is loaded with two traditional humbuckers, a wrap-around bridge and a three-way toggle switch.

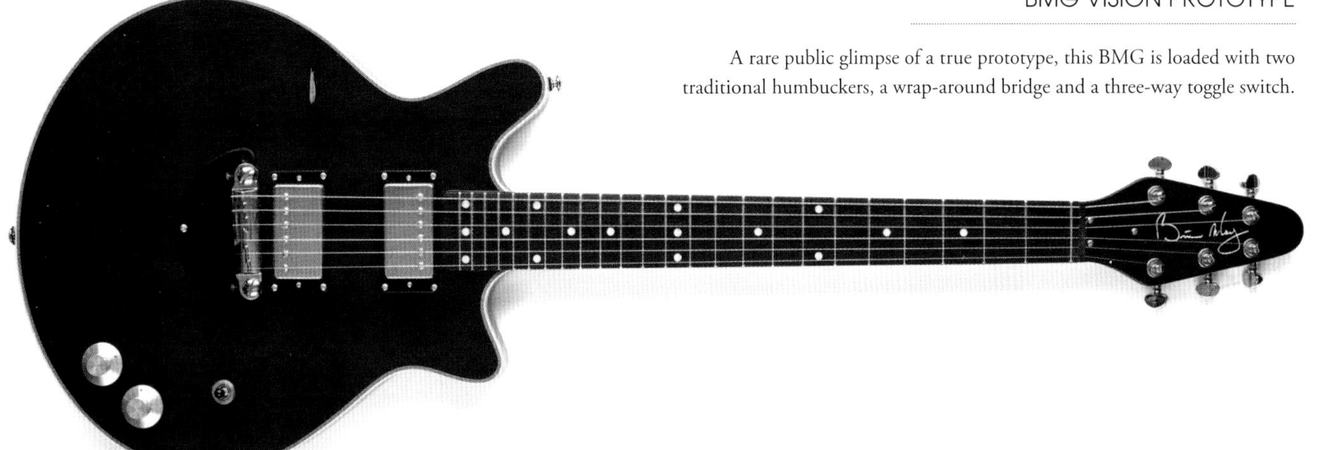

FRYER "JOHN"

One of the three superlative guitars made by Greg Fryer, 'John' was presented to Brian in 1997. It served as Brian's main spare for several years, and remains a firm favourite, along with its brother, 'George'. 'Paul' remains in the possession of Greg, its maker.

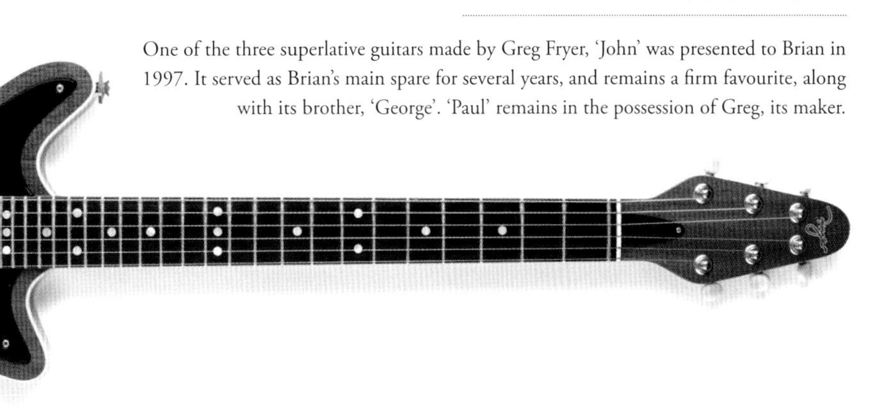

GUYTON GREEN SPECIAL

One of just ten examples made by luthier Andrew Guyton, who's based in Suffolk, England. Brian uses this guitar a great deal and the authenticity of the build is impeccable. On the 2014 USA Queen + Adam Lambert tour, it was the designated 'dropped D' instrument for "Fat Bottomed Girls".

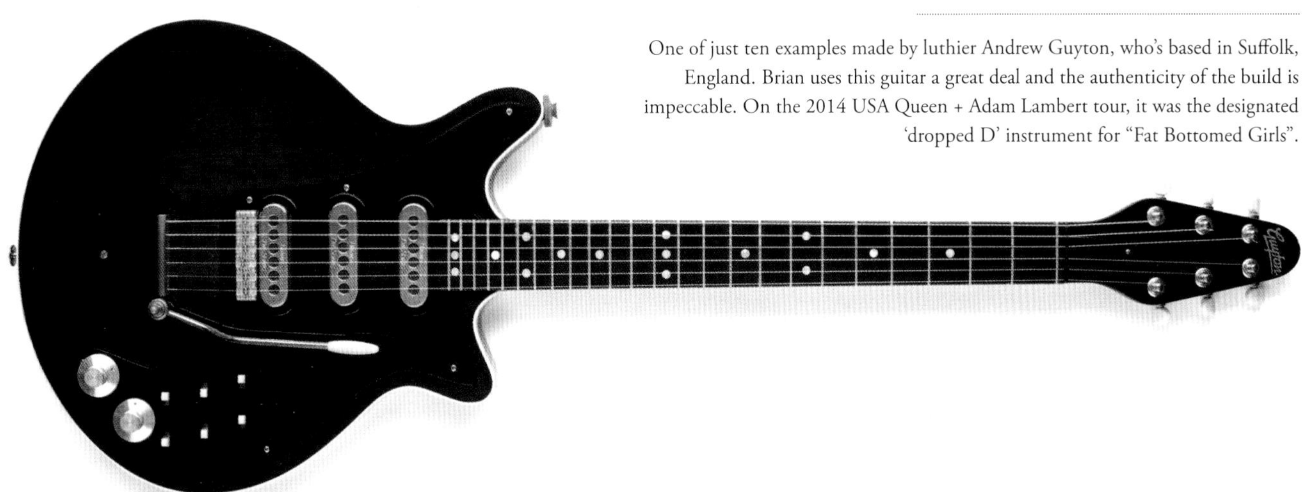

GUILD BM031

A rare member of the Guild Brian May range, with a humbucker in the bridge position alongside the familiar Tri-Sonic single coil.

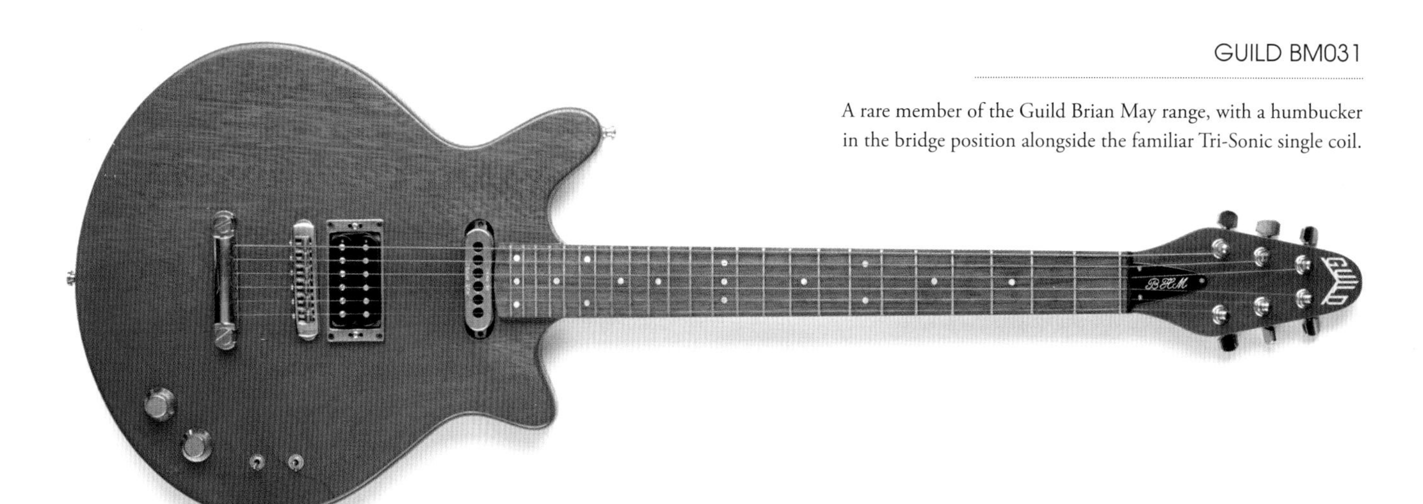

BURNS BRIAN MAY SIGNATURE PROTOTYPE

One of the many production prototypes of this popular guitar, one that married an authentic construction with an affordable price tag.

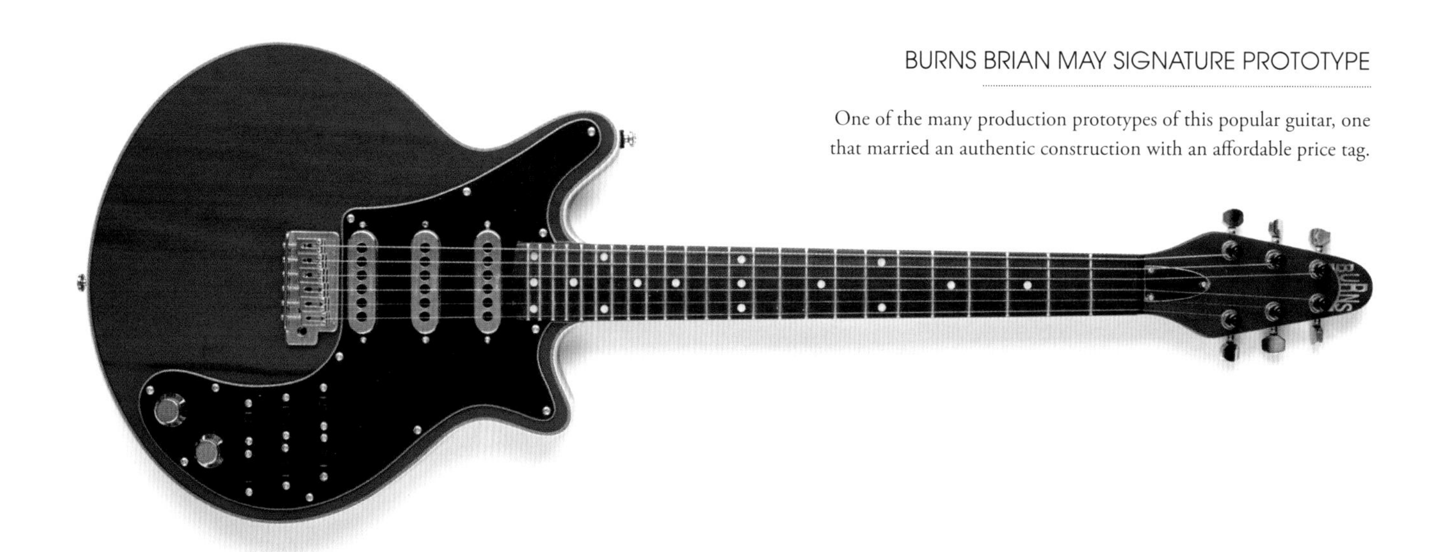

BURNS BRIAN MAY SIGNATURE

The Burns Brian May was launched in 2001, whereupon it received largely positive reviews. Fans, for the most part, loved it. The relationship was dissolved at the point when Brian decided to go it alone with Brian May Guitars, in partnership with Barry Moorhouse.

GUILD BM01

One of a limited run of Brian May signature models reissued by Guild in 1993. The company first tackled the issues involved with producing a commercially viable Red Special with the BHM-1 in 1984, and included DiMarzio pickups and a Kahler tremolo system into the spec. The relationship came to an end after policy disagreements over spec updates.

GUYTON DOUBLE-NECK

"While I was doing the RS Replicas, I kept designing new ideas and different permutations," explains Andrew Guyton. "One of them was the double neck, but initially Brian didn't think he'd ever use it. But then I had a customer come into the workshop, and he saw the drawing and said, 'You build it, I'll buy it.' Brian said yes in principle as long as he could have the first one, which is fair enough."

KZ SUPER BLACK

An uncommon example of Japanese builder Kazutaka Ijuin's work, a Super in black. Queen drummer Roger Taylor owns this guitar, a present from Brian.

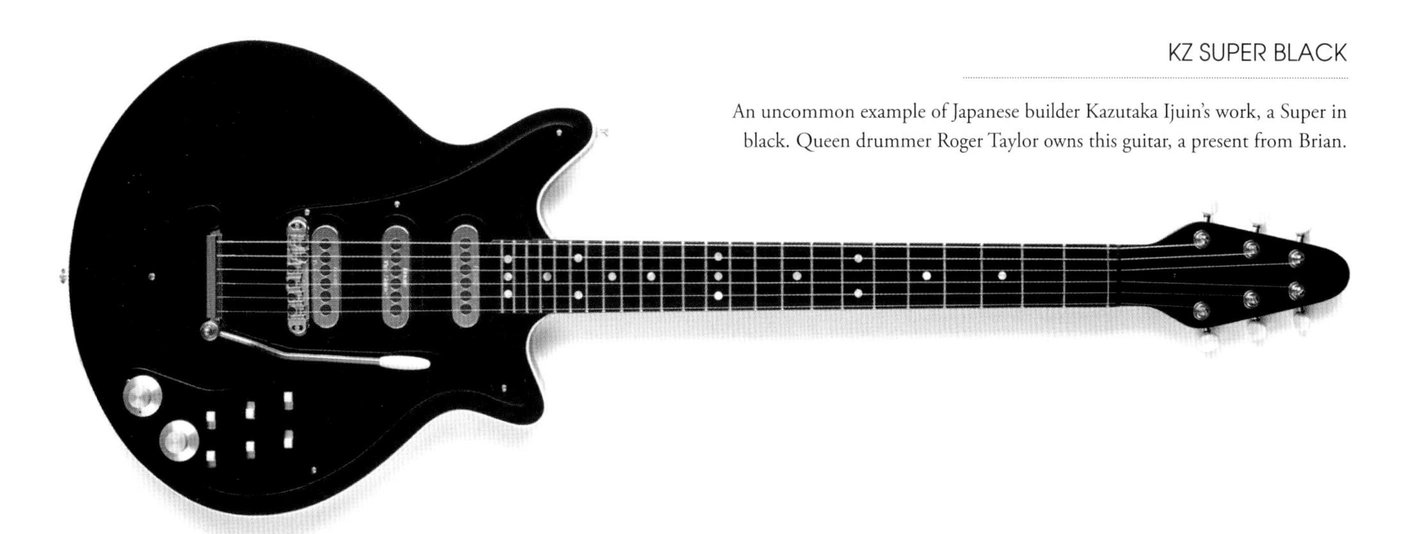

KZ SUPER RED

So good are the KZ Red Special Replicas that this classic red version featured in Brian's live guitar rack from time to time.

BECKNELL METAL SPECIAL

A stainless steel version of the Red Special by American luthier Dwayne Becknell. The body is made of laser-cut stainless steel, with a carbon fibre and hard rock maple neck. The guitar was commissioned by Brian's great friend, guitarist Paul Crook. Brian keeps this guitar tuned up a few semitones, and consistently used it for two songs each night on the 'Acoustic By Candlelight' tours with Kerry Ellis in 2013–14.

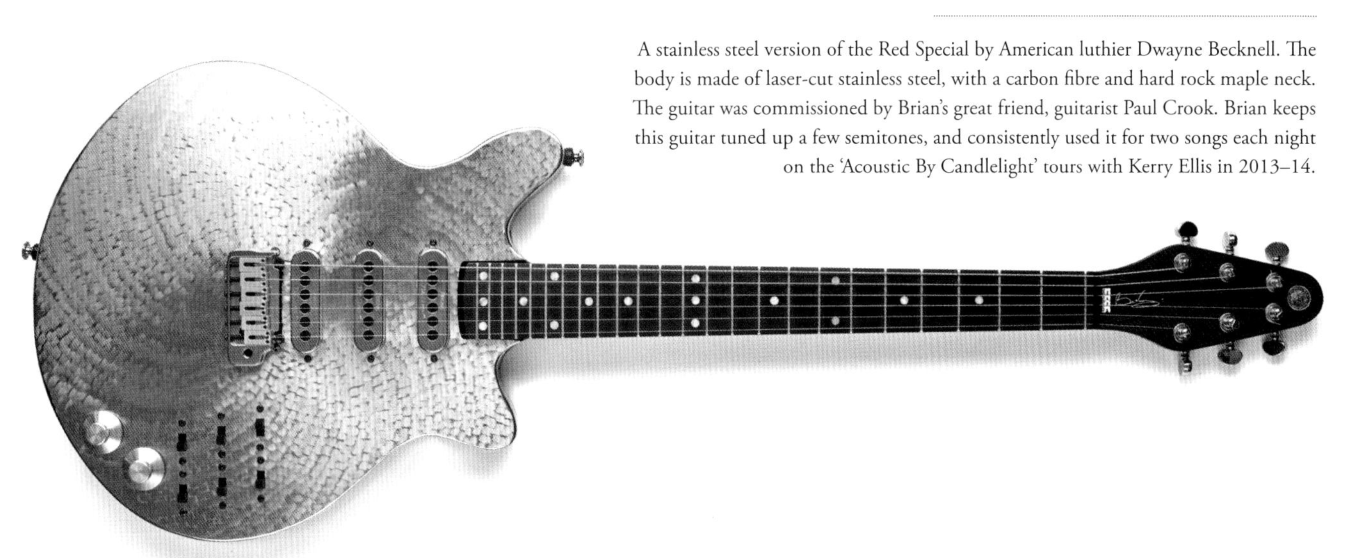

JOHN BIRCH COPY

The first and probably most talked-about of all Red Special replicas, the John Birch was the main live backup to the Red Special during the late 1970s/early 1980s. Most of the work on it was actually done by John D., well-known also for his custom work for Black Sabbath's Tony Iommi. It famously appeared in the accompanying videos to "We Will Rock You" and "Spread Your Wings", before meeting an accidental ignominious end at a show in New Jersey in 1982. However, the pieces survive to this day!

THE SPADE

Built by Andrew Guyton from an early design by Brian. “The idea for this guitar was originally conceived nearly 50 years ago,” says Andrew. “While going through various drawings and photos relating to the Red Special, Brian uncovered early sketches of The Spade, which was to be the second guitar he and his father were to build. However, so successful was the first guitar, that the second guitar was never built.” Until now, that is.

ACKNOWLEDGEMENTS

Photographic credits

The publishers would like to thank the following sources for their kind permission to reproduce the pictures in this book.

Every effort has been made to acknowledge correctly and contact the source and/or copyright holder of each picture and Carlton Books Limited apologises for any unintentional errors or omissions, which will be corrected in future editions of this book.

Brian May Archive: 10, 15, 16, 18, 19, 20t, 20m, 20b, 22, 23, 25, 28, 30, 31, 32, 33, 34, 36, 37, 38–39, 45, 48, 63, 64t, 72l, 80–81 (with thanks to St. Bartholomew's Hospital, London), 86, 111, 112, 113, 114, 115, 116, 117, 118, 119, 120–121, 122b, 123, 124, 125, 126–127.

Harold May: 9, 21, 26–27, 86.

Brian May's personal archive photographed and scanned by Richard Gray and Denis Pellerin.

Corbis: 96–97 Neal Preston/Corbis, 99b Neal Preston/Corbis.

James Cumpsty/Future Publishing: 8.

Duck Productions Ltd: 90 Richard Gray.

Arthur Edwards © 2002: 108, 122t.

Greg Fryer: 76, 77, 78, 79.

Getty Images: 4 Kevin Winter/Getty Images for Clear Channel, 12 Archive Photos/Getty Images, 13t Fox Photos/Getty Images, 13b Michael Ochs Archives/Getty Images, 14t Val Wilmer/Redferns/Getty Images, 14b Rex/Alan Messer, 88 Geoff Dann/Redferns/Getty Images, 93t Fin Costello/Redferns/Getty Images, 93b Rex/Andre Csillag, 94t George Rose/Getty Images, 94b Brad Elterman/FilmMagic/Getty Images, 95, 98 Waring Abbott/Getty Images, 99t Kevin Cummins/Getty Images, 100 Denis O'Regan/Getty Images, 104 Junko Kimura/Getty Images, 105b Franck Fife/AFP/Getty Images, 107 Tiziana Fabi/AFP/Getty Images.

Richard Gray: 2, 17, 20l, 35, 40, 43, 44, 49, 51, 52, 53, 54, 55, 56, 57, 59, 61, 62, 64b, 65, 66, 67, 68, 69, 70, 72r, 73, 74–75, 128–143.

Andrew Guyton: 46, 47, 71m, 71b, 82–83, 84.

The London Stereoscopic Company: 87.

Photoshot: 101 Photoshot/Tony Mottram/Retna.

Queen Productions Ltd: 24 Neal Preston, 102–103 Neal Preston.

Queen Theatrical Productions Ltd: 105t.

Queen Touring Ltd: 106 Christie Goodwin.

Rotosound: 75t.

Michael Sherer: 7.

Thanks to Barry Moorhouse at Brian May Guitars, Roger Taylor, Pete Malandrone, Richie Anderson, Brian 'Jobby' Zellis.

Publishing credits

Editiorial Manager: Roland Hall
Art Direction: Richard Gray
Designer: Russell Knowles
Additional research: Greg Brooks (Queen Archivist) and Gary Taylor
Carlton Books' Picture Research: Steve Behan
Editorial: Malcolm Croft
Production: Rachel Burgess

Queen Management: Jim Beach
PA to Brian May: Sara Bricusse
Queen archivist: Greg Brooks

Red Special breakdown at Allerton Hill on October 8, 2013; performed by Andrew Guyton and Nigel Knight under the supervision of Pete Malandrone; photographed by Richard Gray.

Brian May interview with Simon Bradley filmed at Allerton Hill on August 1, 2013; set conceived by Pete Malandrone and Richard Gray; set built by Russell Barker; interview filmed by Simon Lupton; film crew: Russell Fisher, Malcolm Targett and Bart Baker; equipment by Zero db.

Simon Bradley would like to thank:

Pete Malandrone; Richard Gray; Denis Pellerin; Andrew Guyton at Guyton Guitars; Nigel Knight; Adrian Turner at Adeson pickups; Tim Mills at Bare Knuckle pickups; Andrew Morgan at A-Strings; Greg Brooks; Greg Fryer; Sarah Clark, David Mead and Joby Sessions for guidance and encouragement; Sara, Sally and all at Duck Productions; Ranton and all at *Guitarist* magazine; Roland Hall and all at Carlton Books; Anja Bradley for everything; and to Brian and Harold May, without whom neither this book nor some wonderful music would have been possible.

www.brianmay.com
www.brianmayguitars.co.uk
www.londonstereo.com